OEDIPUS

Oklahoma Series in Classical Culture

OEDIPUS

THE MEANING OF A MASCULINE LIFE

BY

THOMAS VAN NORTWICK

UNIVERSITY OF OKLAHOMA PRESS
NORMAN

Also by Thomas Van Nortwick

Somewhere I Have Never Travelled: The Second Self and the Hero's Journey in Ancient Epic
(New York, 1992, 1996)
(ed., with Judith Hallett) *Compromising Traditions: The Personal Voice in Classical Scholarship*
(New York, 1996)
Excerpts from "Antigone" by Sophocles, "Oedipus at Colonus" by Sophocles,
"Oedipus the King" by Sophocles, from THREE THEBAN PLAYS by Sophocles,
translated by Robert Fagles, translation copyright © 1982 by Robert Fagles. Used
by permission of Viking Penguin, a division of Penguin Books USA Inc. Excerpt
from THE ILIAD OF HOMER, translated by Richmond Lattimore, copyright © 1951
by The University of Chicago, reprinted by permission of The University of Chicago.
Excerpts from THE GIFT by W. Lewis Hyde, reprinted by permission of Random
House, Inc., and by permission of Georges Borchardt, Inc., for the author.

This book is published with the generous assistance of the Kerr Foundation, Inc.

Library of Congress Cataloging-in-Publication Data

Van Nortwick, Thomas, 1946–
Oedipus : the meaning of a masculine life / by Thomas Van Nortwick.
p. cm. — (Oklahoma series in classical culture ; v. 22)
Includes bibliographical references and index.
ISBN 0-8061-3009-1 (alk. paper)
1. Sophocles—Characters—Oedipus. 2. Greek drama (Tragedy)—History and
criticism. 3. Oedipus (Greek mythology) in literature. 4. Masculinity (Psychology)
in literature. 5. Sophocles. Oedipus at Colonus. 6. Sophocles. Oedipus Rex.
7. Men in literature. I. Title. II. Series.
PA4413.07V35   1998
882'.01—dc21   97-40655 CIP

Oedipus: The Meaning of a Masculine Life is Volume 22 of the
Oklahoma Series in Classical Culture.

Text is set in Centaur with display in Lithos.
Text design by Alicia Hembekides.

1   2   3   4   5   6   7   8   9   10

For Mary

Nothing is better and stronger,
than when a man and woman,
joined in their thoughts,
keep a home together

Homer,
Odyssey 6. 182–184

CONTENTS

PREFACE

Indeed, the world is not unlike a vast, shapeless Rorschach
blot which we read according to our inner disposition, in
such a way that our interpretations say far more about ourselves than about the blot.

Alan Watts, *Nature, Man and Woman*

This book focuses on a tenacious pattern of responses to the
world and its meaning, which I find dramatized in two Greek
dramas by Sophocles, *Oedipus Rex* and *Oedipus at Colonus*. My
choice to write about these particular works of art reflects a
reciprocal process: I was preoccupied with the shape of a masculine life as it might be reflected in literature; I thought that
Sophocles' two plays, since they cover such a long period in
Oedipus's fictive life, might give a unique view of the issues I was
thinking about. I was not disappointed, and in fact reading the
plays taught me much more about the meaning of a masculine
life than I could have foreseen before reading them from this
perspective.

The form of this book reflects that initial interplay. I will
pass over some aspects of the plays that classical scholars would
consider crucial to a full understanding of them as Athenian
drama. At the same time, I will try to be open to Sophocles' way
of telling the story so as not to miss, by tuning in too precisely

to my own metaphors, nuances that would enrich my understanding of a masculine life. The analogy I have in mind is a Mozartean interplay of voices: Sophocles tells me a story, I tell it back, and in the process there emerges, I hope, a third story, with its own particular harmonies.

Though I am looking at patterns of growth and perception that I believe are common, in one form or another, to many people, and so will not hesitate to use "we" in talking of modern analogues to the Oedipus myths, I am also in search of the meaning of a particular masculine life, my own—behind the "we" is always the story about me. I am a middle-aged, North American, white male professor, twice married, who feels some kinship with Oedipus. The details of my story are not important here. Let it be enough to acknowledge that in telling Oedipus's story (or Sophocles' version of his story, or my version of Sophocles' version . . .), I am also telling my story, and this means I am seeing the plays through a particular lens.

The lens is, for instance, "gendered." The patterns of emotional and spiritual development I will be tracing through Sophocles' metaphors is one that the Greeks tended to see as biologically based and characteristic of the male sex. This view has been, until quite recently, tenacious in modern cultures: most of the contemporary studies of adult development that apply to the model I see dramatized in Sophocles' plays are based on a male population. But these days there are many who insist that much of what the Greeks saw as biological is actually *cultural* in origin, that what we label "masculine" behavior is not confined to—or only appropriate to—men, or "feminine" to women. The connection of these categories to biology might in fact be seen as sanctioned by those in a particular culture who have some interest in their being understood as a part of "nature," and therefore not to be opposed.

I agree to some extent with the recent skepticism about what is "natural." Indeed one of the definitive aspects of my own middle age has been recognizing the "feminine" parts of myself. Still, I cannot quite understand all gender difference as unrelated to sexual difference. "Understand" here has two meanings: I cannot work out, in a detached, intellectual way, the dynamics of development through midlife, particularly the realization then of contra-sexual elements in the psyche, if adult development is entirely independent of biology. At the same time, my story keeps superimposing itself over the "facts" of the issues, and I am a man—a man who cannot sort out what is biological and what is cultural in my own response to the world. I am inclined for these reasons to talk about "men" here as the principal modern recipients of the ancient heroic myth I describe, but with no great confidence that what I say might not apply in some way to women as well. In any event, I hope that what I say will be of interest to women as well as men, however their expe riences might reflect those of Oedipus.

These qualifications aside, my aim in this book is neither to demonstrate any particular theory about gender and human behavior nor to write a disguised autobiography. Instead I want to look at how Sophocles' two plays about Oedipus dramatize the Greek male hero's evolving struggle to find meaning in his own life, and how that struggle reflects on the meaning of some modern lives, including my own, as felt from within. The key to what I will be after is in two relationships: between feeling that you are authentically yourself and feeling powerful, and between feeling powerful and finding meaning in the world. My reading will draw on modern ideas about adult development and on some enduring spiritual paradigms. Studying both of Sophocles' plays, and seeing them as forming a continuum of sorts, will allow us to add a further dimension by considering how these various relationships evolve as we grow older; pursuing this question through these particular topics, we reinforce a fundamental assumption that guides my search: any inquiry into "the meaning of life" made by a fallible mortal is always intimately bound up with how that person sees the world from within; how we *find* the meaning of life depends as much on who we are and where we are looking from as it does on what is "out there."

The encounter I suggest, between ancient texts and modern life, calls for some delicate balancing. While we will not be recreating the "original" meaning of the plays in Periclean Athens, much of what we say about their impact in the present rests on the work of classical scholars who have tried to recover the original context for performance; while we will be attending as closely as we can to the exact form of the plays as the basis for whatever they may mean to us, we will also be moving back and forth across the boundaries from literature to life so as to think about what the art of fifth-century Athens might say about us and our world.

All of the above suggests that we are looking at the plays through a complex set of filters. It cannot be otherwise, given my goals, and it may be that we will lose focus at times. Still, I prefer to be open about my perspective and its vagaries, erring on the side of disclosure rather than presenting a misleading aura of objectivity. The metaphors I will be developing are to some degree subjective; and others must finally decide for themselves how, or whether, they find their own story in the fictive life of Oedipus. I hope that what I say here will be of interest to classical scholars, but I am also hoping to converse with anyone who wants to think about how and what we can learn about a masculine life from Sophocles' art. For those who want to read more about the issues raised here, at the back of the book I append suggestions for further reading, with a section for each chapter. My recommendations focus on books in English that I have found particularly helpful and relevant to my subject. The bibliography, which follows "Further Reading," refers only to these works and does not begin to cover the immense amount of material written on the Oedipus plays. The particularly intrepid student will find references in the books I do cite to scholarly articles and other specialized studies.

I will be glad if my readers are encouraged to go back and read the Sophoclean plays in their entirety. With that in mind, I quote the translations of the plays made by Robert Fagles—the well-known, easily available *Sophocles: The Three Theban Plays* (New York: Penguin Books, 1984)—rather than my own; those who read Greek need no direction from me.

Because Greek is more compressed than English, Fagles's line numbering does not correspond to Sophocles'; in my references, I use the numbering of the Greek text to which I have referred: Dain and Mazon, *Sophoclé* (Paris, 1955 [1967]). Fagles reproduces the numbering of his Greek text (which is very close to mine) at the top of each page of his translations. For the quotations from Homer's *Iliad*, I have used Richmond Lattimore's version, *The Iliad of Homer* (Chicago: University of Chicago Press, 1951).

I wrote the first version of this book while on a research leave from the Oberlin College in 1992–93. Its contents reflect many hours spent happily talking with my students there and with Nathan Greenberg and James Helm, my colleagues in the Classics Department. Karen Barnes has helped me to prepare the manuscript and has been a constant source of support in other ways. All those mentioned have had a major, positive impact on the book and its author, and I thank them.

The following people have seen all or part of the book in earlier versions and helped me to think through the ideas in it: Andrew Bongiorno, Norman Care, Judith deLuce, Mark Edwards,

Thomas Falkner, Kathleen Norris, Kirk Ormand, Kenneth Reckford, Susan Ford Wiltshire, and the anonymous referees for the University of Oklahoma Press. Working with the Press has brought me into the benign sphere of Kimberly Wiar and Sarah Nestor, my editors there; their support and expertise have been invaluable. The attentions of all of these people have made the book better.

I also want to acknowledge here the friendship and insight of men with whom I have talked about the relationship between life and art over the past ten years. They have been an important part of the book and of my life: Philip Belzunce, Gerald Freedman, Bob Harrist, Bill Hood, Ted Lardner, Kenn McLaughlin, Bill Rudman, Scott Smith, Bill Van Nortwick, John Van Nortwick III, Aubrey Wertheim, and Grover Zinn. Two men in particular were on my mind all through the process of writing the book: my stepfather, Joseph Newton (1905–1984) and my father John Van Nortwick, Jr. (1910–1988). Each in his own way was my teacher, and I miss them both.

Finally, I want to acknowledge a special group of people in whose company I lived while writing this book. I spent the academic year 1992–93 in Akron, Ohio, a vastly underrated city. While there I was fortunate to spend much time in the company of David Kyvig and Christine Worobec, colleagues and friends to whom I talked about Oedipus, masculinity, and myriad other topics, all to my great delight and benefit. I will always think of them when I see this book. I was in Akron because my wife, Mary K. Kirtz, is Professor of English and director of Canadian Studies at the University of Akron, and it was her turn to have a short commute. Spending every day with her, talking about my ideas and hearing hers, simply basking in the warm glow of her intelligence and grace, created a matrix of fruitful energy in which my work and my life flourished. The book is dedicated to her with love.

OEDIPUS

INTRODUCTION

Therefore those who govern by intellectual knowledge can hardly maintain a nation; this is possible only for those who unite with the great harmony and keep natural responsiveness.

Wen-Tzu, *Understanding the Mysteries*

You know how he left this spot, of course,
you saw him go. No friend to lead the way,
he led us all himself.
Now, when he reached
the steep descent, the threshold rooted deep
in the earth by the great brazen steps, he stopped . . .

Oedipus At Colonus 1587–1592

So Oedipus, aged and blind, takes his last walk on this earth, out of the world of this play, off the stage of Athenian drama. Suppose we could stand with him, as he pauses in the grove of the Eumenides just before he completes his mysterious exit, and look back over the fictive life he has led in the two plays written about him by Sophocles. We would see, some distance away, the most familiar story in all of ancient literature, of the man who killed his father and fathered children with his mother; in the near distance, the sequel, with Oedipus now nearing death, a

3

wandering outcast but somehow reanimated as he comes closer
to the gods.

Behind the figure of the old Oedipus, we might see the
penumbra of Sophocles himself. Born near the place we are
standing, he lived past ninety but never saw this, his last play,
produced; a story reported by Cicero—perhaps apocryphal,
perhaps not—tells of how the playwright, like Oedipus, quar-
reled and broke with his sons in his old age (*De Senectute* 7.22). So
when Oedipus turns again and walks out of sight into the embrace of the "kindly goddesses," we may imagine his creator
going out with him, taking a last bow. We are left behind, to
consider the afterlife of the two plays.

Here we encounter a marked divergence. The first play becomes, even in the next fifty years, a paradigm against which
much prior and subsequent drama will be measured. The problem of Oedipus's guilt or innocence, the role of "fate" in his life
and trials, the riddles of blindness and insight, the reflections of
childhood sexuality in his story, all take center stage in Western
cultural life. The last play does not fare so well. While there
have been countless productions of *Oedipus Rex* over the centuries, *Oedipus at Colonus* appears much less frequently; the early
Oedipus is the best-known figure in ancient drama, his older self
a more obscure presence; critics, beginning with Aristotle, rank
Oedipus Rex at the top of Athenian tragedy; about *Oedipus at
Colonus* opinion varies.

Such rankings will not concern me here. Rather, I want to
look at the way the two plays fit together, and especially how
they trace a life. The end of *Oedipus Rex* has seemed to many if
not most people to illustrate the typically indomitable Sophoclean hero, self-destructive but somehow admirable in that very
quality. The static, essentially futile qualities in this kind of hero
do not carry as much weight, however, if we view the end of *Oedi-*

pus Rex as part of a larger developmental cycle: Oedipus is not at
the end of his greatness but only at the beginning of a long
struggle to realize the fruits of self-blinding. Looking through
Oedipus Rex and beyond, to Sophocles' last play, we see in the
blind old man evidence of an entirely new way of seeing himself
and the world, a perspective that subsumes and transcends the
earlier, tragic, vision.

The life that is formed by joining the two plays dramatizes
fundamental questions about human existence that troubled the
Greeks and endure in our own time: Who am I? How do I become the person I am to be? How much of myself and my life
do I make and how much is made by forces beyond my control?
Using other terms, we might say that Oedipus's life, as it appears
in Sophocles' plays, raises issues about (1) the nature, knowledge, and realization of the self; (2) the relation of that self to
the cosmos outside it. By thinking about the plays, we will also
be led to a richer understanding of how these topics are inter-
related: how we make real our authentic self presupposes that we
know what that self is and can therefore recognize it when it appears; as we feel more authentically ourselves, we feel more powerful in the world, and this in turn seems to give life meaning.

The length of Oedipus's fictive life in Sophocles' dramas gives
us the chance to think about a further complexity: our ideas
about ourselves and our place in the larger scheme of things
change as we grow older; when we are young and heroic, to
"make" ourselves seems not only possible but obligatory; by the
time we enter middle age, our encounters with the hard realities
of life have usually tempered that early certainty, and if we live
into old age, the evolution continues. Modern studies of the life
cycle have asserted that there are certain crucial points in the
process of growing up when our notions about who we are and
where we fit are challenged by experience. These studies further

suggest that how we meet those challenges, with denial or acceptance, with despair or energy, may determine in large part whether we thrive and grow in what life remains to us. It is my contention that Sophocles, like all great artists, grasped all of this, and gives us in his Oedipus plays a subtle and rich portrait of the process of growing up and growing old.

The Hero Story and the Cosmic Order

These issues are my focus, as they emerge from the dense fabric of the drama and as they persist today, perhaps carried by different vehicles but vividly present. In Greek literature up to Sophocles' time, the characteristic venue for exploring relationships between the masculine self and the world was the heroic narrative, a story that, in its most basic shape, shows the hero's struggle to impose order on an unruly cosmos. Notice that by ordering the universe, giving it a shape, the hero imparts meaning: formlessness is experienced as meaningless. We may press the model further: insofar as the hero is able to impose his will on the world and others in it, he feels powerful; as his sense of empowerment grows, he feels that he is fulfilling his role in the world, or, to put it another way, he is becoming the person he is supposed to be. And, finally, as he achieves a sense of agency and its accompanying sense of personal authenticity, the world shows to him a pleasing orderliness: life has meaning. The relationships in this perspective are complex and sometimes slippery, but for our purposes it is enough to note that in this view a meaningful life depends on seeing shape and order in the world, and in feeling a sense of agency within that order.

In some narratives, this model is tested but ultimately reaffirmed. Odysseus undergoes temptations and trials, struggles against hostile forces in the world, angry gods, fairy-tale monsters, greedy suitors, but finally reasserts himself as father, husband, and king in Ithaka. In doing so, he reestablishes both the orderly universe he left when he went to Troy and his own identity (and power) within it. It is more characteristic of the Greek imagination, however, to conceive of the hero story from a "tragic" perspective, to focus on the challenges to heroic empowerment inherent in the world as they saw it. Here the emphasis is on the finality of death, the one force a mortal hero can never overcome. If we had to sum up the message of Greek tragic literature in one sentence, it might be: What does it mean to be a creature who knows he must die? And this question suggests a paradox: limits give shape and therefore meaning to life, but also challenge agency, and so diminish the potential (in this way of seeing) for creating meaning by imposing one's will on the world.

From the brute fact of mortality followed a preoccupation with other dimensions of a limited human existence, the gods, the world of nature, the mysterious workings of fate and chance. Deities reinforce the contours of human experience by contrast. Looking, acting, and talking more or less like mortals, they are nonetheless all-knowing, all-powerful, ageless, and, most distinctly, immortal. Since nothing can change what they are, the lives of the gods within their perfect world are both carefree and without limit (or form); thus, in the heroic perspective, they are ultimately meaningless. Within their little society the gods quarrel, threaten, and sulk, but we can never be moved (except maybe to laughter), because on Olympus, nothing matters. But when they intervene in the human world of death and change, the acts of the omnipotent gods become enormously significant. Divine will, in the world of mortals, becomes as baffling and invincible as death—a force that defines human life by its irresistible strength.

Necessity appears in other, less anthropomorphic forms in the Greek cosmos reflected in heroic narratives. Each person's life was shaped by a "destiny," or "fate," and by the intrusion of chance. Though parallel to divine will in the ultimate surety of its fulfillment, fate was often understood to be independent of the gods, personified by three sisters who spin out the thread of a person's life to its destined end, then cut the thread. Chance could sometimes be thought of as an element of randomness subsumed within the larger necessities of fate or divine will, or, rarely and more frighteningly, as an independent force.

Within the mutable world of mortals, human life was further distinguished from other life forms, akin to humans in their vulnerability to death but still essentially other. Human civilization was often defined by the Greeks as against the world of nature, including the other living but nonhuman creatures: human knowledge and skill combine to control the world of nature so as to shape it for human use. Sophocles himself gives one of the most vivid portraits of this view in *Antigone*:

> Numberless wonders
> terrible wonders walk the world but none the match for man—
> that great wonder crossing the heaving gray sea,
> driven on by the blasts of winter
> on through the breakers crashing left and right,
>   holds his steady course
> and the oldest of the gods he wears away—
> the Earth, the immortal, the inexhaustible—
> as his plows go back and forth, year in, year out
>   with the breed of stallions turning up his furrows.
>
> And the blithe, lightheaded race of birds he snares,
> the tribes of savage beasts, the life that swarms the depths—
> with one fling of his nets
> woven and coiled tight, he takes them all,
>   man the skilled, the brilliant!

He conquers all, taming with his techniques
the prey that roams the cliffs and wild lairs,
training the stallion, clamping the yoke across
  his shaggy neck, and the tireless mountain bull.
And speech and thought, quick as the wind
and the mood and mind for law that rules the city—
  all these he has taught himself
and shelter from the arrows of the frost
when there's rough lodging under the cold clear sky
and the shafts of lashing rain—
      ready, resourceful man!
         Never without resources
never an impasse as he marches on the future—
only Death, from Death alone he will find no rescue
but from desperate plagues he has plotted his escapes.

(332–363)

The heroic drive to control the cosmos, to channel its power
for human civilization, is clear enough here. Note especially the
role of human intelligence as the instrument of control, a major
theme in *Oedipus Rex*. Characteristic, too, is the opposition between images of linear, human progress, marching through time,
and the circular, ever-renewing rhythms of nature. But finally,
death itself is the most "natural" of forces, and gives the lie to
human claims of power over nature. The polarity of time/time-
lessness now comes back in a less friendly form: the ultimate
limit of human time is death.

The exact parameters and hierarchies of these various forces
within the cosmos varied according to the imagination of the
narrator and the shape of the narrative. For our purposes here,
the point to grasp is that each force was perceived as imposing
a limit on human power. Here we return to the paradox of lim-

its and to the tragic potential in the heroic myth. Human life is
informed, shaped, by limits imposed from without. One "meaning" of such an existence would be in terms of these limits: I am
a creature that occupies a certain space for a certain time within
the larger cosmos. Yet the tragic hero's idea of himself is as an
imposer of order on the world—an agent. While this role need
not necessarily conflict with the larger order, the tragic hero always challenges the limits of human existence; he defines himself as powerful and authentic insofar as he appears to overcome
them. In short, he imagines himself a god.

So it is that ancient heroes often have one divine and one
mortal parent. Living by the facts of their birth on the boundaries of human and divine, they transgress, challenging the limits of human existence, and in particular the limit of mortality.
Achilles, son of the goddess Thetis and the mortal Peleus,
presses in various ways against the boundaries of humanity, and
only achieves some measure of maturity and reintegration with
his fellow mortals after accepting the loss of his friend Patroclus—and, by extension, accepting his own mortality. In his
conciliatory speech to Priam at the end of the *Iliad*, he defines
human existence by the fact of death, as against the immortal
gods:

Such is the way the gods spun life for unfortunate mortals,
that we live in unhappiness, but the gods themselves have no
    sorrows.
There are two urns that stand on the door-sill of Zeus. They are
    unlike
for the gifts they bestow: an urn of evils, an urn of blessings.
If Zeus who delights in thunder mingles these and bestows them
on man, he shifts, and moves now in evil, again in good fortune.
But when Zeus bestows from the urn of sorrows, he makes a failure

of man, and the evil hunger drives him over the shining
earth, and he wanders respected neither of gods nor mortals.

Iliad 24. 525–533

We see here in the poem a recognition of the futility of the
heroic will to control the world like a god, to see unlimited
power as the validation of our authentic existence as humans.
Rather, Achilles now understands himself as part of a larger
whole, over which he has only limited control; he, like all mor
tals, must die.

Sophocles, as we will see, dramatizes the heroic impasse in a
similar way in *Oedipus Rex* The "fall" of Oedipus at the end of
the play is represented by the actors and chorus onstage as un-
relievedly dark—a total ruin. Yet from another perspective, one
that we will explore, Oedipus, like Achilles, "descends" from divinity to humanity: he becomes what and who he always was
though he did not know it. That this ought to be seen as disas-
trous, horrifying, is only evident if we accept the heroic illusion
of limitless power to begin with. Our reading will see the story
of Oedipus as one in which defeat becomes the emblem of salvation, darkness brings light, birth follows from death—one in
which mortals pursue the "right" thing for the "wrong" reason.

Oedipus Rex, rich and complex as it is, offers a version of the
hero story that is in some sense familiar. Not so *Oedipus at Colonus*,
which takes us into undiscovered country. Now the "hero" of
the play is a very old man, lacking the usual heroic attributes of
youth, physical vigor, and aggression. From these departures follow others: the aged Oedipus is powerful not because he imposes
his will on the world but because he is about to leave it; far from
defying the power of the gods, he wants only to bring his will
into phase with divine will. The late Oedipus is previewed to
some degree in Sophocles' *Philoctetes*, as *Antigone* rehearses some of

the scenes of *Oedipus Rex*, but finally nothing is quite like *Oedipus at Colonus*. Not only does the play extend and enrich the heroic myth, it also dramatizes, like its predecessor, fundamental issues about the relationship between the self and other. Taken together, the two plays about Oedipus form a continuous whole, through which Sophocles weaves a dense and subtle picture of how a human life may evolve, moving from disharmony to harmony with the larger rhythms of the cosmos.

The Tragic Perspective in Sophocles' Time

While Sophocles' themes in the Oedipus plays drew on ancient mythic patterns, they were also vividly contemporary. The fifth century B.C. in Athens was a time, like our own, when old models for the place of humans in the cosmic scheme were under intense scrutiny. As the older, aristocratic oligarchy gave way to Peisistratus the tyrant in the sixth century and then to what the Athenians called democracy, familiar assumptions came into question: about the relationship between divine will and human excellence, between inherited abilities and those that could be learned, between what was "natural" and what was a product of the human mind. The Sophists, essentially traveling teachers, challenged old ideas, and claimed to be able to give their students access by their teaching to the kinds of excellence that had been thought to be strictly a product of nature. In such a climate, questions of personal identity, self-realization, and empowerment were bound to be central.

Sophocles lived in the midst of this ferment, as a citizen and as an artist. His medium, tragic drama, is informed by a fundamental tension between the world of the heroic myths, which provide most of the stories on which the playwrights draw, and the intense, rapidly evolving intellectual and social life of democratic Athens. This tension may account for one major differ-

ence between tragic drama as a genre and the epic poetry in
which many of the heroic stories first appeared. Epic tends to
resolve the issues raised in the course of the narrative, or at least
to achieve some kind of closure, however tenuous. Though
Odysseus's urge to wander seems dangerously active, we nevertheless leave him firmly in place as master in Ithaka; the re-
sumption of war looms over the end of the *Iliad*, but Priam and
Achilles do reach a spiritual resting place and bring the poem's
major themes to completion. While dramatic trilogies like
Aeschylus's *Oresteia* may present some degree of resolution (and
even here we are unsure, since Aeschylus's work is the only example surviving intact) single plays almost never suggest closure.
It is much more characteristic for tragedy to expose rifts in the
structure of life than to suggest how they might be made whole.
Even when resolutions are imposed by the deus ex machina in
some late plays of Euripides, the wild discrepancy between the so-
lutions effected and the realities dramatized in plays undermines
any confidence we might have in the newly reformed cosmos.

Oedipus Rex is no exception. At the end of the play, Oedipus
has been blasted out of his former self and faces a blank future.
It is not even made clear whether he will be exiled from Thebes.
Nothing in the last lines looks forward in any direct sense to
Oedipus at Colonus, which will not appear on the Athenian stage
for more than twenty years. Continuities, nevertheless, are obvious. We leave Oedipus in Thebes at the end of his youth, blind
and accursed, begging to be exiled; he reappears near Athens as
an old, blind exile, led by his daughter Antigone. The central
theme of the famous riddle that Oedipus solves in the earlier
play is the life cycle of a man, from infancy, to vigorous adulthood, to enfeebled old age. Oedipus thus leaves the stage toward
the end of phase two and walks back on at the end of phase
three. The last play, like its more famous predecessor, addresses

themes of self-realization and the relations between knowledge, will, and power. It is hard not to see Sophocles—by this time himself on the threshold of death—returning to his most vivid creation to see him out of this world. And if the two Oedipus plays offer a more complete picture of the life cycle, nevertheless that last walk into the grove of the Eumenides leaves the old man on another mysterious threshold, with many questions left unanswered.

Modern Metaphors

When we look for the relevance of Sophocles' metaphors for our own lives, we are most likely to be peering through the lens of psychology. Questions about personal identity, about the inner dynamic that drives us to act in one way as young adults, another as we age, about how we experience the encounter with forces beyond our control, all have been framed most often, in the last two-thirds of this century, in the discourse of psychology. Psychological metaphors have in fact so permeated our common parlance about human behavior that we often no longer recognize their source. The ascendancy of this model has much to do with the enthronement, in the twentieth century, of scientific inquiry, and much of the writing on behavior is heavily technical and based on clinical observation of patients. Looking for the meaning of Oedipus's life in our time, I will often use the language of psychology, but in doing so I make no claims for the primacy of this way of describing human behavior. In my view, psychologists are no closer to understanding the mysteries of human life than Sophocles: they just have a different set of metaphors, which resonate more vividly in our modern heads than other metaphors sometimes do. This being so, I am happy to avail myself of them, but not with the purpose of validating Jung's perspective over that of Sophocles. In my view, both thinkers are approaching the same dilemmas in human life, the same questions, and responding to them with different descriptive metaphors. I, in turn, borrow from both (and from others) to offer my own set of metaphors.

The first, and most famous psychological analysis of *Oedipus Rex* was, of course, Freud's, and later work on the play from this perspective abounds. But these investigations, focusing as they do on how specific acts in Oedipus's life reflect what Freud saw as the universal pattern of psychic evolution in male infants, are not directly relevant to our project here. Modern psychological work on the adult life cycle begins rather with Jung, who was the first to recognize the midlife transition as crucial to adult development. Indeed, Jung was virtually alone among early psychologists in showing *any* interest in the psychological development beyond adolescence, and his metaphors are still the bedrock on which all modern studies of adult development rest.

The fundamental aspect of Jung's work (in this case, a refinement of Freud's original model) for our purposes is the division of the human psyche into the conscious and the unconscious. The former, directed by the "ego," is what we experience as our "rational selves," driven by the will, our name for the desires governed by the ego. The unconscious is the home of all psychic material not available to the conscious mind, but active nonetheless, influencing behavior below the level of consciousness, appearing in dreams, or projected onto the world around us. For Jung, life is an unfolding process, in the course of which we work to achieve a harmonious balance between the conscious and unconscious mind. As we age, the inner springs that feed our perception of ourselves and the world change; what works well for us as teenagers can be toxic in middle age; reaching an apparent dead end in our evolving journey toward death, we can choose to turn and walk out another way. The key to health in this perspective is acceptance of what our inner darkness is telling us about ourselves, followed by the long process of integrating the new versions of ourselves that follow from this acceptance into our conscious idea of who we are. Seen through this lens, a life is never doomed, either by the workings of malevolent or indifferent powers beyond human reach or by a "mistake" made in haste or the heat of passion. Rather, different stages of a person are born, mature, and then give way to their successors, the process being made easier to live through by an openness to change and a certain curiosity about what is hidden. Openness, patience, flexibility, and curiosity in the face of things unknown—all these are qualities I want to cultivate in the reading that follows, and so I find Jung a compelling guide.

Jung departed from Freud in seeing the unconscious as divided into the *personal* unconscious, repository of all material repressed by the ego out of consciousness, and the *collective* unconscious, where "archetypes"—psychic structures common to the human race, genetically transmitted and encoded—reside. This latter aspect of Jung's model has been the most controversial, and is still viewed with suspicion by many. It suggests that we all share a common set of psychic templates, which predispose us to respond to the world in certain ways. The existence of archetypes probably cannot be "proved," because, as Jung imagined them, they are not material, cannot be seen. The validation of the theory of archetypes must rather be in their explanation of human behavior. It is not necessary to our aims here to prove or disprove the validity of Jung's theory of archetypes, even if I were competent to do so. Let it be enough to say that I find the theory appealing insofar as it offers a model for understanding the continuities in human behavior between Sophocles' world and ours. (Needless to say, the more one views gender differences as culturally rather than naturally generated, the more troubling the theory of archetypes becomes.)

Looking at the life course as it is reflected in Oedipus's life, we will be borrowing a few psychological metaphors in particular. It is a common human habit to think of the conscious level of the self as the whole self: "I" am essentially my ego, and the parts of me not available to the conscious mind are then denied or projected out onto others. Jung's notion of the unconscious "shadow," containing all the things about me that my conscious mind finds unacceptable and perhaps frightening, is a prominent model for understanding the tendency to project. In this model, I project the shadow onto some other person (or group), who then becomes the vehicle for some part of me that I am unable to accept. Now I can respond with proper fear or disapproval to all these qualities, since they are not "me." Ancient epic poetry shows a story-pattern that can be understood in terms of the shadow—the story of the hero and his companion, with the latter objectifying parts of the hero that the hero is unable to accept. Patroclus can be seen as this kind of figure in relation to Achilles. The death of Patroclus becomes in this model the final result of Achilles' denial of what he represents, and the spiritual healing that Achilles experiences at the end of the poem is, in part, the result of his finally accepting as his own what Patroclus embodied.

Jung's metaphor for what Achilles undergoes at the end of the *Iliad* is called individuation. It was Jung's contention (again, working from Freud) that the self can be understood as a mechanism that seeks equilibrium of all its parts, so that if one element is denied its proper power in the conscious mind, it becomes more powerful in the unconscious, usually making trouble in return on the conscious level. Jung further saw it as the goal of all persons to work over the course of their lives toward an accommodation between the various parts of the self. This process entails bringing unconscious material to consciousness and then acknowledging it as our own, and so integrating it into our idea of who we are. Integration takes all of our lives, since certain parts of ourselves become accessible to us only after we have reached a certain point in our evolving life course. But always, as Jung saw it, the goal of all persons is to seek wholeness, to complete ourselves. Self-realization is, then, self-completion.

It is characteristic of the tragic hero to exemplify the tendency to mistake the ego for the self. This myopia finds expression in the extraordinarily willful behavior of the tragic hero, accepting no limits, going too far: the ego is firmly in control here. In the Oedipus of *Oedipus Rex*, we find a striking form of this distortion, which brings out forcefully its implications for our struggle to achieve first self-knowledge and then self-completion. The person Oedipus thinks himself to be is not only an incomplete version of the real man, but even in some senses a false one. Oedipus is, in a particularly vivid way, a self-created person, and one created—through no fault of his own—on false premises. As the play progresses, we see the increasing strain and momentous consequences of Oedipus's alienation from his true self. Finally, in the last scenes, the rift is made plain, and Oedipus is forced to confront a version of himself that has been entirely unknown to him.

The "new" identity of Oedipus can be understood as embodying unrealized aspects of the self that had been denied access to the consciously fabricated version that ruled in Thebes. In this sense, as we will see, the first play ends with Oedipus on the threshold of what characteristically occurs for men in our time and place around the middle of life. He is, then, in a position to begin the painful and protracted struggle of accepting and then integrating the new parts of himself, as a prelude to the second half of life.

We have seen that one consequence of the hero's myopia is a tendency to mistake himself for a god. If he moves beyond this stage to an acceptance of his mortality, he is able to see himself in a new relation to the rest of the cosmos, to step (or be driven) down from the plane of divinity to that of humanity. This new perspective, which we call humility, now allows (or forces) the hero to accept the possible existence of transcendent powers in his world, and so opens the way to a new element of spirituality in him: now that his identity is not dependent on being without limit, he can envision himself more comfortably as part of a larger whole. From this perspective may flow in turn a new way of configuring the relation between identity and empowerment. This is the phase of life that *Oedipus at Colonus* explores for us.

Modern studies of aging are often structured by the division between two basic roles for older men. In one, which is characteristic of modern, postindustrial societies, the old are devalued because their age prevents them from being "productive" in the way they were when younger and stronger. The underlying assumptions here ought to be familiar to us as students of the heroic myth. To be powerful, and so productive, is to be an active agent in the world—young, strong, Achillean. The other model, most often associated with what we now call "traditional" cultures, sees the old as powerful in a different way. Being closer to death, they are closer to the gods, and so they become numinous, possessing numen, or supernatural force. Notice here that the old are powerful not because of what they *do*, but because of who and where (in terms of the life cycle) they *are*. This second perspective also accords influence to the old because of their experience, which gives them "wisdom." But one suspects that the real force behind this deference is respect for the power of the gods, however the society may imagine them: traditional societies, like modern ones, are driven by power issues, but the sources of power are imagined differently.

Notice, too, that the traditionally powerful old man implies a conception of the boundaries of the self that follows from the heroic "descent" to humanity. The hero is powerful insofar as he imposes his will on the world, defying the limits imposed by the power of transcendent forces. We have seen that this stance is characteristic of the person who mistakes the ego for the self. The old man is powerful because he occupies a particular place in the larger order, which is thought to put him in touch with transcendent forces. He is powerful not because he defies limits but insofar as he harmonizes his will with the order of the cosmos. One consequence of this shift, which we will explore in detail later, is the possibility of expanding the boundaries of the self—of identifying with what the young hero can think of only as separate from himself. The last hours of Oedipus on the Athenian stage and on this earth dramatize this new configuration of self-in-the-world with a richness found nowhere else in Western literature.

1

SELF-CREATION AS SELF-DESTRUCTION

Oedipus Rex I

> . . . a *young* person . . . is not yet at that point in the rhythm
> of mortal time where he is ready to give up. He is set to
> continue as a matter of biological necessity, for the action
> of living requires "follow through" like the blow of the
> hand upon a drum: it aims beyond the skin.
>
> Alan Watts, *Beyond Theology*

OEDIPUS:

> Oh, my children, the new blood of ancient Thebes,
> why are you here? Huddling at my altar,
> praying before me, your branches wound in wool.
> Our city reeks with the smoke of burning incense,
> rings with cries for the Healer and wailing for the dead.
> I thought it wrong, my children, to hear the truth
> from others, messengers. Here I am myself—
> you all know me, the world knows my fame:
> I am Oedipus.

(1–8)

The most famous of ancient plays begins in pain and fear. As
Thebans die from the plague that has inexplicably fallen on
them, the air is thick with smoke, from offerings to the gods,
from burning corpses. In his opening words to the pathetic

group of suppliants, Oedipus invokes images meant to reassure. As ruler, he is a father to Thebes and its citizens, and like a father he will take care of his "children." We see already the supreme self-confidence and ease of command in Oedipus, who can address not only other people's children as his own, but also be a father to men older than he is. But beyond even this there is, in the wretched posture of the citizens, the hint of prostration before a deity. We are "clinging to your altars," says the priest in reply (15–16): *his* altars? We discover, some 950 lines later, that these altars are actually those built to worship the god Apollo, but at this moment the confusion is telling. Oedipus strides onstage firmly in the role of civilizing hero, ready to defend the city against disorder—trouble that is carried in this case by a seemingly unmotivated sickness that takes people off without regard to their merits. That he also exudes a *godlike* mastery in the eyes of his subjects only strengthens the heroic portrait: the people are complicit in his desire to see himself as without limit.

Sophocles wastes no time, then, in establishing Oedipus in the category of hero. After a cautious qualification—they know he is not *really* equal to the gods, but first among mortals—the suppliants invoke the parallels between this situation and the one Oedipus faced when he first came to the city, the siege of the Sphinx (35–39). Once again, the hero confronts a mysterious threat to Thebes—a problem that must be solved. Like the Sphinx and her riddle, the plague is powerful, tricky, inscrutable; its defeat, like hers, calls for the application of reason as an instrument to control disorder. At the same time, a second, ironic dimension of the action is available to those who know the whole story: the "fatherhood" of Oedipus, symbolic of his power to control, is in fact deeply ambiguous, built on a self-created history that will not hold up in the light of what he dis-

covers in the course of the play. Oedipus is leading, in his ignorance, a double life.

The different titles for the play that have come down to us
sum up the duality. The Greek title, *Oedipus Tyrannus*, uses a word
that had a specific political meaning in Sophocles' time. A
"tyrant" meant a ruler who took power on the force of his deeds,
not because of any hereditary claim to the throne. (Whether the
word had the strongly negative tone in Sophocles' time that it
later came to have is unclear.) The Latinized version, *Oedipus Rex*,
uses the Roman word for a *hereditary* ruler. In his Corinthian persona, as an outsider who wins power through his heroic acts,
Oedipus is a "tyrant"; when the facts of his birth become
known, he becomes a "king" (the Greek word for this is *basileus*).
So either title is appropriate, though one points to the early
Oedipus, the other to the later figure; passing from the earlier to
the later recapitulates Oedipus's own passage from outsider to
insider, from stranger to citizen, and, on another level, from
hero to polluted outcast.

Oedipus goes on to express his care for the city in another
potent metaphor:

> My children,
> I pity you. I see—how could I fail to see
> what longings bring you here? Well I know
> you are sick to death, all of you,
> but sick as you are, not one is sick as I.
> Your pain strikes each of you alone, each
> in the confines of himself, no other. But my spirit
> grieves for the city, for myself and all of you.
> I wasn't asleep, dreaming. You haven't wakened me—
> I have wept through the nights, you must know that,
> groping, laboring over many paths of thought.

After a painful search I found a cure:
I acted at once.

(58–69)

Again the fragrance of divinity surrounds the hero, as he becomes the agent of Apollo, the god of healing, looking after his sick "children." And again, the inflation is tinged with irony, since it is Apollo who, by bringing him to confront his buried self, will finally reveal to Oedipus the extent of his own spiritual sickness. But this truth will be available to the hero only after more pain; for the moment, Oedipus remains the masterful doctor, who stays up nights thinking and thinking until he finds a cure. Characteristically, the discovery brings immediate *action*—the sending of Creon to Delphi to consult the oracle of Apollo.

A good ruler, Oedipus consults the gods to help his city. As the suppliants note, a god also supported his earlier intervention to defeat the Sphinx:

> We taught you nothing,
> no skill, no extra knowledge, still you triumphed.
> A god was with you, so they say, and we believe it—
> you lifted up our lives.

(37–39)

We have seen that the hero's tendency to press against the limits of humanity implies a misperception of his power in relation to that of the gods. Here we might suppose that the model of the hero as transgressing limits is softened, qualified, that the earlier hints of a divine aura around the ruler are countered by his willingness to defer to divinity. Perhaps, but the passage above suggests we proceed with caution. Though the chorus mention a god, the extent and nature of the involvement are vague: the Greek phrase for "A god was with you," *prostheke theou*, could be rendered, "with a god as prop." In any event, the suppliants' attention focuses on what *Oedipus*, unaided by any special instruction or prior expertise, did with the support. The word rendered "lifted up," *orthosai*, always contains the meaning "to straighten": the hero restores order, straightens up what has become crooked, disorderly. The role of the gods in the life of Oedipus is a complex one, evolving through the course of both plays. For the moment, we can say that the emphasis remains on Oedipus as self-created, self-taught, self-reliant, imposing his formidable will and knowledge on the world to serve his city and his "children."

The Intellectual Hero

We may pause to reflect on the particular form that Oedipus's heroism takes. Though he is apparently a stout fighter, having killed (we will discover, or perhaps already know) several men on the road from Delphi to Thebes, Oedipus's principal strength is intellectual. He defeated the Sphinx by his wits, not with brawn; to rescue the city from plague, he stays up all night *thinking*; the entire play turns on what Oedipus knows and how he comes to know it. Odysseus is the first Greek hero to survive by relying primarily on his wits, and Sophocles' Oedipus is his descendent. But the form of the *Odyssey* is, as we have noted, basically comic, in that the emphasis is on restoring the status quo, and the limitations of Odysseus's way of coping with the world are not emphasized. Oedipus is the first *tragic* intellectual hero, part of a story that reveals and explores the darker aspects of his kind of heroism, the desire to control the world by imposing order through the structures of the intellect.

Those of us who make a living primarily by thinking can perhaps recognize something of Oedipus in ourselves. As children, we were taught that knowledge brings power, that being ignorant makes you vulnerable to manipulation by those in the know. And in this century, heroic mastery of the world through intellect has become the guiding metaphor for Western cultures: nuclear physicists channel the power of life's most basic structures to light cities or obliterate them; the astronauts, modern heroes going where ordinary people cannot, bring back arcane knowledge for the benefit of all. As I write, I participate in the myth in my own way. By "analyzing" the plays, I impose my own structure on Sophocles' drama, and draw a "meaning" from this ordering: the heroic critic or theorist is much with us in the academic world. This is not to say that all intellectual structures are hubristic—hardly a practical view—but only to note the *potential* for self-aggrandizement and loss of authenticity in the seemingly "objective" work of scholarship. And the further analogue is also clear: Oedipus's alienation from his true self has its counterpart in the anxiety and spiritual malaise so prevalent in our own time.

The Hero and His Community

The opening scenes raise another important issue, the problematic relationship between a hero and his community. Of Oedipus's devotion to Thebes there seems no doubt: he will do anything to relieve the suffering; while others are in their own private pain, he grieves for the entire city. And yet, the self-assertion we see in Oedipus, fueled by a persona that is both self-created and alienated from fundamental aspects of his nature, has much in common with the pride of Achilles, which drives the latter into isolation from his community of warriors and goads him into sacrificing their lives to serve his fiercely individual sense of honor. The tragic hero's impulse to defy limits, to impose his will on the world, runs counter to those qualities of cooperation and humility that bind members of a community together. Although, as in the case of Oedipus, the hero's power *can* be harnessed for the good of a community, the bond is by definition precarious, and could be ripped apart by the hero's will at any time.

The connection between alienation from self and harming the community is straightforward in the case of Achilles. His blindness to the qualities in himself that Patroclus embodies leads him to leave the Greek army, an act that inevitably brings destruction for his fellow warriors. Oedipus, as we have seen, has no desire to abandon his city; he is full of pain at the suffering of its citizens. And yet, the plague that is killing Thebans is, as he and we will soon discover, the result of his ignorance about himself: he would not have killed his own father knowingly. Here we encounter a central aspect of the play's symbolic mode of presenting Oedipus's acts and their motivation: Sophocles presents as external and objective what we might think of as internal and subjective. This tendency pervades the play (and much of ancient literature), and we will be noting it all through our discussion. For now, we may observe that the plague, on one level a concrete instrument of Apollo's will, which is killing people, can also be understood as the externalized sign of Oedipus's internal disorder, his inability to act out of his true nature, which is grounded in facts about his birth to which he is for the moment denied access.

On a larger scale, the plot of the drama externalizes Oedipus's self-scrutiny, a process that in our time might be presented as introspection, a looking inward. At the level of dramatic technique, this strategy powers the biting irony of the play, as Oedipus pursues an enemy who turns out to be himself. At the same time, it preserves the aspects of Oedipus's character that exemplify the heroic vision, the impulse to act *out into* the world, to make it conform to his will. And finally, we see the implications of this perspective for the process of self-realization. By making Oedipus's inner nature something that he thinks of as "out there," Sophocles dramatizes the hero's desire to see himself as the product of his own will shaping the world: the more he seems to bring the world into line with his will, the more powerful he feels; and the more powerful he feels, the more personally authentic he feels. He is creating himself through action.

The Hero and the Life Cycle

The double life of Oedipus, enforced by his ignorance, projects outward what is an inner estrangement, characteristic of young men in our own time, from certain aspects of their nature that they are not yet ready to acknowledge. Modern psychological studies of the life cycle tend to confirm what those of us who work with young adults of either sex already know—that they are often loathe, and even in some sense unable, to acknowledge the limits imposed on them by nature and the society they are entering. When we are told, in our late teens or early twenties, to "make something" of ourselves, by going to college, getting a job, getting married, the message encodes ancient heroic urges—and it seems that we are ready to hear them. Likewise, when at the end of the play Oedipus finally turns to face his buried life, he takes a step we must take at the end of our youth, when our inner nature seems to make us ready for the next part of our lives.

Daniel Levinson and his colleagues, who produced the first comprehensive psychological study of the adult male life cycle (Levinson 1978), have shown that the tendency, characteristic of the hero, to see himself as self-created finds its modern analogue in what they have called the "formation of the Dream" by young males making the transition from late adolescence to early adulthood (56–58, 71–111). The Dream, as Levinson puts it, is a "vague sense of self-in-adult-world" (91). Leaving the family, separating from parents, must be followed by the formation of some kind of provisional sense of identity as an adult. The connection between separation and identity is fundamental. Separating from his parents in late adolescence, the young man replays a part of his infancy, when he first discovered that he was biologically different from his mother and began to sense that in this difference lay the key to his own identity as an autonomous being. The resonance of infancy in adolescence helps to account for the strong urge in young adult males to think of leaving home as an occasion for the formation of a new, autonomous identity. This is the time when nature conspires with culture to make young men devalue the parts of themselves that follow from their genes—their connection to their parents, but also, by extension, their very mortality: the Dream must be pursued by a new, heroic person. Though, as we will see, a man's susceptibility to this natural and cultural bias changes later in life in response to his evolving sense of who he is, contemporary ideas in Western society about what makes for "the good life" are not so flexible. As Levinson puts it: "Humanity has as yet little wisdom for constructing the portrait of the hero as a middle-aged man" (215).

I have said that the heroic perspective implies a particular understanding of the relationship between identity and empowerment. David McClelland has studied how people experience power from the inside in various cultures (McClelland 1975) and his findings are helpful in understanding the relationship between feeling powerful and feeling *authentic*, having a firm identity, in the early adult period. McClelland distinguishes categories of experiencing power according to the *source* of power and its *object* (14). In the first stage, most clearly identified with infancy, power is experienced as coming from outside oneself: the source is "other"; the object is oneself. In the second stage, both source and object are felt to be oneself: we gather knowledge, for instance, and so "give" ourselves power. In stage three, we are the source, but we express power outward, directing it to some other object. Finally, in stage four, we feel ourselves to be part of a dynamic for the flow of power in which we are neither source nor object: we somehow serve to facilitate the training of power from outside ourselves onto some object that is not ourselves.

Though McClelland sees all these modes as present to some degree in everyone at all periods of life, he has found some trends in the relative influence of each at various stages of life and in different kinds of cultures. Stages one and two emphasize the *accumulation* of power, three and four its *expression*. The former pair are more characteristic of Eastern cultures, the latter of Western. That is, Western cultures tend to understand power more readily as a function of its *expression*, whereas Eastern cultures can accommodate more easily the notion that one may be powerful without expressing it outside of oneself. We can also see how the four stages might characterize movement through the life cycle, from dependency on other powerful beings to the accumulation of power through learning and experience, to the expression of power by influencing others, to the final stage of serving the expression of powers beyond oneself.

Stage three is clearly the heroic mode of experiencing power. While we might see Oedipus as also representative of stage two, given the importance of knowledge as the basis for his power, the emphasis in the play itself is on his expression of the intellectual power he has accumulated: Oedipus is above all a man of *action*. It is interesting to note that McClelland had some difficulty in finding evidence of outlets for stage four expressions of power, with its implicit devaluing of egocentric behavior, in modern Western cultures: we have an underdeveloped societal framework for understanding how a person can express power without being the source of the power. As it happens, *Oedipus at Colonus* addresses this very problem, and is one of the few artistic expressions of what McClelland calls the most mature realization of personal empowerment.

The name of Oedipus sums up much of what we have been saying. The etymology of the name in Greek is probably from *oideo*, "to swell," plus *pous*, "foot," referring to the piercing of his feet when he was exposed as an infant. But there is also a punning reference—the Greeks loved puns—to the verb *oida*, "to know," making Oedipus "know-foot." (No one in the play seems to be aware of this second meaning of Oedipus's name: the double entendre is for the audience's benefit.) What we see is that, like the two titles for the play, the two meanings for Oedipus's name form a shorthand version of the plot. The riddle of the Sphinx asked what creature goes first on four feet, then two, then three—the answer being humans. When Oedipus then, in his Corinthian, heroic persona, solves the riddle and conquers the Sphinx, he is "he who knows feet," or the hero who conquers disorder through knowing. Now Oedipus's introducing himself in the first scene to the citizens who already know him seems less peculiar: he has come to rescue them again, as he did when he conquered the Sphinx, and his very name records the first victory.

Because his name can, in this etymology, be the product of his first heroic *act*, as far as he and the citizens of Thebes can know it, there is also the sense, in the introduction, of Oedipus *creating himself* again for us through action: like all heroes, he thinks of himself as the product of the imposition of his will on the world. For this naming-as-self-creation we have a famous precedent in Oedipus's heroic predecessor, Odysseus. The journey of Odysseus back to Ithaka from Troy is informed by a cyclical rhythm, as the hero repeats the pattern of arriving as a stranger in a strange land, withholding his name while establishing himself in the new milieu, and then triumphantly announcing his name when he feels safe enough to do so. The moment of revelation is always a charged one in the poem, as Odysseus completes the journey from unknown, anonymous stranger to the most famous and powerful of heroes. And each cycle builds toward the final triumphant return in Ithaka, when Odysseus returns to his previous status as husband, father, and king.

In each of these episodes, there is symbolism that suggests that Odysseus not only returns to his old self, but that he is *reborn*. By announcing his name to the Phaeacians in book 9, he marks the end of an interlude that begins with his being washed ashore naked and defenseless, like a newborn infant (*Odyssey* 5. 394–398); earlier he escapes from the womblike cave of the Cyclops by disguising himself as Outis, which means Nobody; the pains that the Cyclops feels after his eye is poked out are described with the word the Greeks used for birth pangs; pulling away from shore, he completes the process by announcing his name gleefully (and almost prematurely) to the Cyclops (*Odyssey* 9. 216–564); his final rebirth comes just before he slaughters the suitors and takes control of his household, as he goes from being disguised as a withered old beggar to glorious, invincible warrior (*Odyssey* 22. 1–4).

In each case, Odysseus begins in anonymity, and it is only through his actions that he gathers the power that certifies his identity. Identity follows from action, in the typical heroic way: Odysseus creates himself through action, and the more powerful he is, the more *himself* he is. This is precisely the dynamic that *Oedipus Rex* dramatizes, but through different means and in a tragic, rather than comic, context, which exposes the limits of such a way of understanding oneself in the world. When Oedipus symbolically celebrates his self creation through heroic action by naming himself at the beginning of the play, a second, ironic, level is carried in the etymology: he is "know-foot," but he is also "swollen-foot." He will create himself again through his actions in the rest of the play, but the identity he brings to light will be based on facts of his birth over which he has no control. One of the most compelling aspects of Sophocles' dramatic vision is the way in which Oedipus's heroic actions, of which the hero is so proud, bring him into an arena where they are impotent.

The God's Voice

The hero is vividly drawn, and the plot moves forward, driven by his restless energy. Now the voice of Apollo begins to sound ever more articulately in Thebes, modulating from the echoes of plague sufferers, to the report of Creon, to the words of the god's own prophetic surrogate, Tiresias. As the information about the plague's origins grows more explicit, we see the double life of Oedipus come slowly into sharper focus. Under the pressure of events, Oedipus pushes ever harder to end the sickness, but the duality of the play's thematic structure turns his actions back on themselves: training his sights on the enemy outside, he is pursuing his own destruction; acting out of his heroic persona, he is searching for a "truth" that is blocked by the denial implicit in the structure of that very persona.

Creon arrives from Delphi with concrete advice: the oracle orders the Thebans to "[d]rive the corruption from the land" (98). Characteristically impatient, Oedipus presses: What is the source? How can they purify themselves? The cause of the plague, Creon now reveals, is a murder. Of whom? The former king, Laius, who was killed on the road by "murderers" who must be killed or exiled. Now energized by the prospect of *acting* to correct the problem, Oedipus intensifies his questioning and the details come out. Laius was killed on the way back from Delphi, where he had consulted the oracle; all the potential witnesses were also killed, except one, who was not much use, telling them only that the murderers were "thieves"; the Thebans were prevented from pursuing the killers by the appearance of the Sphinx, who "persuaded us to let the mystery go/and concentrate on what lay at our feet" (130–131).

Certain details repay our attention. First, there emerges a famous crux: Creon reports that Apollo's orders are to "pay the killers back" (107). We will discover, if we do not already know the story, that Oedipus acted alone when he killed Laius, so the plural "killers" is puzzling. Can the god have lied to Creon? Is Creon changing the story consciously, or perhaps unconsciously? We never find out, and the confusion shields the real killer until late in the action. Meanwhile, the Sphinx reappears, and the timing is also puzzling. Who is the creature, and why does she appear just when the Thebans are about to go after the murderer of Laius? And how is it that she "persuades" the Thebans to attend to her riddle instead of the seemingly more pressing matter of finding the king's killer? Again, we never find out: the Sphinx remains mysterious.

But what we do know is telling enough. The Sphinx is a strange, hybrid creature, usually represented in art as a winged woman with a lion's hindquarters. She sings her riddles like a poet: the suppliants call her the *skleras aoidou* (harsh bard) (36); Creon calls her *poikiloidos* (singer of riddling songs) (130). The verb used to describe how she turns the Thebans toward her riddles is *prosagomai*, which most often is descriptive of mild inducement, not forceful constraint—something appropriate, we might say, for a singer. We might be reminded, in fact, of the Sirens, the singers of seductive knowledge that Odysseus encounters on his

adventures. Their songs are so alluring that men cannot resist
their pull, and Odysseus has himself lashed to the mast of his
ship in order to listen safely.

The phrase "what lay at our feet" (131) is a literal translation
of a Greek idiom meaning what is immediately present, underfoot, and echoes Oedipus's use of *empodon* (underfoot) in his asking what got "in their way" so that they did not pursue the
killers of Laius. All this talk of feet in the context of the riddle
is striking, and suggests a level of meaning beyond the immediate and practical for the decision of the Thebans. The Sphinx,
a singer who can bind an entire city with her songs ("sphinx" is
from the same root as the verb "to choke," and her songs are art-
ful structures that challenge the intellect) arrives just at the right
moment to keep the Thebans—and, we might add, Oedipus—
from discovering the truth about Laius and about the heroic
stranger. Instead, both the hero and his adopted city turn toward the challenge of defeating the "singer," which the hero
does by using his formidable intellect to control the Sphinx's
disorderly powers. Both the hero and the city look to "feet" instead of to the facts of blood that bind Oedipus and Laius, that
define the relationship between the killer and victim. Like Oedipus, the city becomes "know-foot." Or to put it another way, the
city joins Oedipus in the formation of his heroic Dream.

Ironically, it is Oedipus who begins the process of ending the
dream, while acting to preserve it:

> No.
> I'll start again—I'll bring it all to light myself!
> Apollo is right, and so are you, Creon,
> to turn our attention back to the murdered man.
> Now you have *me* to fight for you, you'll see:
> I am the land's avenger by all rights,
> and Apollo's champion too.

But not to assist some distant kinsman, no,
for my own sake I'll rid us of this corruption.
Whoever killed the king may decide to kill me too,
with the same violent hand—by avenging Laius
I defend myself.

(132–138)

He is certainly fighting for "himself" here, but our perspective offers, as usual, ironies. The self he fights to preserve is the
self-created hero of the Dream: by acting to control disorder
with his mind, he continues to nurture this persona. But we
know that he is also right in seeing the killer of Laius as a threat
to him. Once the facts of Oedipus's relationship to Laius come
to light, they will "kill" the Dream and its hero.

The chorus of Theban citizens now enter and sing an ode to
the gods. Calling on Zeus, Apollo, Athena, Artemis, and finally
Dionysus, they beg for help against the plague, which they see as
a form of the war god Ares: "the fever, the god of death/that raging god of war." (190–194). It is characteristic of the chorus—
who in Greek tragedy often represent ordinary humanity in contrast to the extraordinary hero—to call abjectly on the gods for
help. They trust their leader, but they also look beyond him: the
limits of human power and will are more comfortable to them
than to the hero.

After the chorus, Oedipus reappears:

You pray to the gods? Let me grant your prayers.
Come, listen to me—do what the plague demands:
you'll find relief and lift your head from the depths.

I'll speak now as a stranger to the story,
a stranger to the crime. If I'd been present then,

there would have been no mystery, no long hunt
without a clue in hand. So, now, counted
a native Theban years after the murder,
to all of Thebes I make this proclamation:
if any of you knows who murdered Laius,
the son of Labdacus, I order him to reveal
the whole truth to me.

(216–226)

True to his heroic nature, Oedipus answers the call for divine
assistance: *he* will be the god's voice. His use of the words
"stranger" and "native Theban" continues, of course, the ironic
doubleness that informs the entire play. He sees himself as *xenos*
(stranger) to those events long ago, as *astos* (citizen) now. We,
however, know he was born *astos* in Thebes and made *xenos* to his
own birth in exile. The alienation reflected in his misperception
and in his attempt to speak for the gods parallels the larger gap
in self-knowledge that drives the plot. The hunt begins in
earnest now, and Sophocles hammers home the ironies in Oedipus's relentless search for himself: The citizens must show no
mercy. They must drive the criminal out; never speak to him;
never shelter him; never let holy water touch his hands. If he
turns out to be part of the royal house, may the curse strike
Oedipus himself. Oedipus is king now, taking the place of the
murdered man, even taking his place in Jocasta's womb, making
him *homosporos*, of the same seed, as the dead king. So Oedipus
will fight as if for his own father (216–275).

Tiresias

The voice of Apollo grows yet more vivid when the prophet
Tiresias appears from Delphi, answering a summons from
Oedipus. The scene that follows is pivotal for our understand-

ing of Oedipus's progress toward self-realization and its implications for our time. The dynamic of the confrontation here, between Tiresias and a willful king, the blind old man telling the
younger ruler that he must yield to the ties of blood to stop the
spread of sickness through the city, appears first in Sophocles' play
Antigone, produced more than a decade earlier but dramatizing
events in the story of Oedipus and his family that *follow* the death
of Oedipus. In that play, Creon, the ruler of Thebes, has impris-
oned Oedipus's daughter Antigone in an underground cave, in-
tending to starve her to death because she has defied his orders
and buried her brother Polynices. Tiresias arrives to tell Creon
that his reading of sacrificial entrails has shown him that something is dreadfully wrong in Thebes: the city is "sick," and Creon
must cure it, by releasing Antigone and honoring the ties of blood
that drove her to bury her brother against the king's command.
Creon defies the old man: like all prophets, he says, Tiresias is driven by greed; *the prophet* is the sick one. Tiresias fights back, re-
minding Creon that he, Tiresias, saved the city from the last
plague (the one to be dramatized by Sophocles fifteen or so
years later in *Oedipus Rex*). Goaded by the king's further insults,
the old man finally reveals a grim prophecy—that Creon's child
will die to pay for the life of Antigone. He then leaves abruptly.

Creon, frightened by the prediction, becomes unsure of his
resolve. At the urging of the leader of the chorus, he rushes off
to release Antigone but arrives too late—she has hanged herself.
He finds his son, Haemon, who is betrothed to Antigone, hug-
ging the corpse. He tries to bring Haemon out of the cave, but
the young lover is beyond this, trying first to stab Creon, then
killing himself. When the news of these events reaches Creon's
wife, Eurydice, she retires to the palace and kills herself with a
knife, cursing Creon with her last breath (*Antigone* 988–1305).

The parallels to *Oedipus Rex* are significant. In both plays, a mysterious sickness grips Thebes—one that turns out to reflect an illness in the king. The issues that inform the argument between Creon and Tiresias are akin to those between Oedipus and the same prophet—the demands of blood ties, sanctioned by the gods, as against imperatives created in the context of human civilization. The emotional dynamic is also the same in both scenes, with the king listening deferentially at first, then lashing out at the prophet when the advice goes against the dictates of his will, the old man in turn growing angry himself, and finally revealing a dreadful secret. In the aftermath, similarities persist: Eurydice's suicide prefigures Jocasta's; Creon, like Oedipus, loses contact with his wife and children through his pride.

We might conclude, then, that Sophocles was drawing on the end of the *Antigone* when he composed the confrontation of Oedipus and Tiresias. But the differences between the two scenes are as significant, for our purposes at least, as the similarities. We note, for instance, that while, in *Antigone*, Tiresias seeks out Creon, and eagerly delivers his advice, in the later play he is called to Thebes by Oedipus, and when he discovers what the king wants, tries to leave without responding:

TIRESIAS:

               How terrible—to see the truth
when truth is only pain to him who sees!
I knew it well, but I put it from my mind,
else I never would have come.

OEDIPUS:

What's this? Why so grim, so dire?

TIRESIAS:

Just send me home. You bear your burdens,

I'll bear mine. It's better that way,
please believe me.

(316–322)

The feeling here is that the prophet realizes that it is not the right time for Oedipus to know the truth, and that he, Tiresias, is not the one to tell it. It will come out, in any event: "What will come will come./Even if I shroud it in silence" (341). What Tiresias knows about Oedipus is profound and definitive for the hero's identity. The prophet's reluctance reflects a fundamental truth about the relationship between self-knowledge and self-acceptance: we can learn certain things about ourselves only when we are ready, emotionally, spiritually, to learn them. Oedipus— as Tiresias senses and we are about to find out—is not ready.

Hot on the trail of the killer, Oedipus has acted to bring aid from the god. Faced with the old man's reluctance, he is incredulous, then outraged, and the insults begin. Tiresias is a traitor—the "worst of evils" (334); *he* has plotted the entire disaster; had the prophet had eyes, *he* would have killed the king. In the face of this attack, Tiresias's resolve to keep quiet is swept away in the anger of the moment:

I charge you, then, submit to that decree
you just laid down: from this day onward
speak to no one, not these citizens, not myself.
You are the curse, the corruption of the land!

(350–353)

Oedipus finds this charge preposterous, and his anger escalates yet further, envisioning now a plot between Tiresias and Creon to overthrow him. The exchange heats up, with the king trying to bully the seer into backing down from his claims, the old man growing more direct: It is Oedipus who is the murderer; he and his loved ones live together in infamy. Oedipus now mocks the old man's blindness and draws a new charge: Oedipus is the one living in ignorance, blind to his own life. Does he know his own parents (415)? A second mention of his parents seems to bring Oedipus up short: "Parents—who? Wait . . . who is my father" (437)? Tiresias has hit a tender spot but is now beyond responding to the change in the king's tone and begins to taunt the king:

TIRESIAS:

This day will bring your birth and your destruction.

OEDIPUS:

Riddles—all you can say are riddles, murk and darkness.

TIRESIAS:

Ah, but aren't you the best man alive at solving riddles?

OEDIPUS:

Mock me for that, go on, and you'll reveal my greatness.

TIRESIAS:

Your great good fortune, true, it was your ruin.

OEDIPUS:

Not if I saved the city—what do I care?

(437–443)

Tiresias is ready to go, but he delivers one more blast of truth as the king moves offstage:

                    I will go,
once I have said what I came here to say.
I will never shrink from the anger in your eyes—
you can't destroy me. Listen to me closely:
the man you've sought so long, proclaiming,

cursing up and down, the murderer of Laius—
he is here. A stranger,
you may think, who lives among you,
he soon will be revealed a native Theban
but he will take no joy in the revelation.
Blind who now has eyes, beggar who now is rich,
he will grope his way toward a foreign soil,
a stick tapping before him step by step.
Revealed at last, brother and father both
to the children he embraces, to his mother
son and husband both—he sowed the loins
his father sowed, he spilled his father's blood!

Go and reflect on that, solve that.
And if you find I've lied
from this day onward call the prophet blind.

(447–462)

A powerful and definitive scene. To grasp the full import of
the exchange, we need to think carefully about what is said, how
it is said, and who says it. The argument shows us some darker
aspects of the king's powerful will. He is used to getting what he
wants, and when Tiresias balks, his rage follows with alarming
speed. The kindly, paternal ruler of the first scene is blown away
by the force of anger, to be replaced by an accusing, bullying
tyrant. We also observe the relationship between fear, denial,
and anger in Oedipus. Faced with information about himself
that he cannot for the moment accept, he reacts by lashing out
at the apparent source, Tiresias, and then Creon. The hero is ac-
customed to creating the "facts" about his own identity by imposing his will on the world. Meeting parts of himself that are
not of his own making, he sees a stranger—someone over whom
he has seemingly no control. The hot denial and projection of

responsibility onto others is unusual in its scope, but like all of the hero's traits it only reflects an outsized version of ordinary human behavior. In this case, we see the familiar imprint of fear, which we often cover with anger, a secondary and more acceptable emotion, one that makes us feel less vulnerable. Projection, too, is a normal reaction to things about ourselves we cannot accept: now we are able not only to escape the responsibility of dealing with the unacceptable parts of ourselves, but also to experience the pleasure of berating someone else and feeling superior.

The accusations that follow Tiresias's revelations fit comfortably with the heroic urge always to act out into the world. Finding an enemy without keeps Oedipus on the offensive, channeling that famous energy in a way that continues to build the heroic persona. The introspection that will lead finally to Oedipus's ironic enlightenment is still transmuted by the plot structure and the operation of denial into an externalized hunt. Achilles again offers a significant parallel. After Hector kills Patroclus, the anger of Achilles, which had been directed at Agamemnon, shifts to Hector, and culminates in his death at Achilles' hands. But Achilles, too, bears some responsibility for the death of Patroclus, in that he sent his friend out into battle disguised in his (i.e., Achilles') armor, making him a conspicuous target for the Trojans. Like Oedipus, he directs his anger outward, toward Hector, rather than inward, as he might just as well have done. In Achilles, as in Oedipus, heroic self-expression works against introspection and self-knowledge. Two exchanges in particular highlight Oedipus's urge to shift responsibility for bad news:

OEDIPUS:
You, shameless—
aren't you appalled to start up such a story?
You think you can get away with this?

TIRESIAS:

I have already.
The truth with all its power lives inside me.

OEDIPUS:

Who primed you for this? Not your prophet's trade.

TIRESIAS:

You did, you forced me, twisted it out of me.

(354–358)

OEDIPUS:

Enough! Such filth from him? Insufferable—
what, still alive? Get out—
faster, back where you came from—vanish!

TIRESIAS:

I would never have come if you hadn't called me here.

(429–432)

In his rage, Oedipus "forgets" that he started the hunt.

Another Oedipus

The figure of Tiresias repays closer scrutiny. The heated exchange with Oedipus shows him to have a formidable will of his own: he is not intimidated by the tyrant's bluster, and goaded out of his initial detachment he trades insults with verve. But finally the differences between Oedipus and the old prophet are more telling. While the king draws all of his sense of identity and power from actively imposing his will outward to effect a sense of control over his fate, Tiresias is a passive conduit for the power of Apollo: he is powerful insofar as he brings his will into phase with the will of the gods, a force over which he has no control. Oedipus pushes always to control by *seeing* the world and *knowing* it; Tiresias is blind. Oedipus finds his truth by projecting outward; the truth "lives inside" Tiresias.

We do not know whether Sophocles might expect his audience to know other stories about Tiresias not mentioned in the play, but one in particular, preserved in Ovid, is tantalizing. Out walking in the woods, Tiresias saw two snakes copulating. He hit them with a stick and was instantly turned into a woman. Seven years later, out walking again, the female Tiresias saw two more snakes intertwined, hit them with a stick, and became a man again. Being the only human who had lived as both a man and a woman, he was now in position to decide a dispute between Jupiter and Juno as to which sex had the greatest pleasure in intercourse. He said women, which did not please Juno, who struck him blind. Jupiter, taking pity, gave him the gift of prophecy as compensation (*Metamorphoses* 3. 314–338). The sexual ambiguity reflected in this story fits with the figure we encounter in *Oedipus Rex*—a man whose identity is defined by traits that the Greeks at least saw as more characteristic of women: passivity, inwardness, a closeness to larger, extrahuman rhythms in the cosmos.

Tiresias is, then, *complementary* to Oedipus, in the way that the hero's companion often is in ancient hero stories. Patroclus embodies qualities that complement Achilles' dominant traits: he is compassionate where Achilles is hardened by solipsism and shows humility in the face of Achilles' overbearing hubris; he suffers when his companions die, whereas Achilles sends them to their death to serve his pride. Enkidu, the companion of Gilgamesh in the Mesopotamian hero story *The Epic of Gilgamesh*, has a similar function. I have said that such figures can also be understood in the context of Jung's metaphor of the shadow, and that the spiritual task of the ancient hero—to accept and integrate those parts of himself that the companion (or second self, as I prefer to call him) objectifies—finds its analogue in Jung's notion of individuation, or self-completion, the process by which humans reach fulfillment or wholeness. The relationship of Oedipus and Tiresias is one of the richest expressions of this dynamic in ancient literature.

The key to Tiresias's potency in the story lies in the close fit between what he *is* and what he *knows*. He is, as I have said, complementary to Oedipus, embodying qualities that Oedipus has lost track of in himself: what he knows or, more accurately, carries within himself is an entirely "new" Oedipus, complete with new birthplace and a new father and mother. True to his "feminine" nature, Tiresias becomes a kind of midwife to the birth of a "new" man, whose identity is in fact prior to the one known in Thebes, a man who has a different past from the Oedipus known to the Thebans and to Oedipus himself, one whose future will be determined by the knowledge of this past.

This new identity will not become real for Oedipus just yet—denial must have its day. But when it does, we will be able to reconstruct from it two different life journeys for Oedipus. The first, which Oedipus has lived out in the eyes of the Thebans and his own conscious mind, is bright with heroic achievement; the second, latent in Tiresias and in Oedipus himself, is full of familial antagonism, violence, and forbidden desires.

In the first life, Oedipus, troubled by the chance remarks of a drunken dinner guest—that he was not his father's son—sets out from Corinth to Delphi, to consult the oracle. Receiving a frightening prophecy—he would kill his father and breed children with his mother—he leaves, determined to avoid Corinth and escape the prophecy's fulfillment. On the road to Thebes, he negotiates a spot of nastiness from unfriendly travelers and arrives in time to defeat the Sphinx with his wits and reap the rewards of his heroism: he rules over the city and enters marriage with the recently widowed queen. He rules well, gathers glory, and fathers children (774–813).

The second life begins at Thebes. Laius and Jocasta, faced

with a threatening prophecy—that Laius would be killed by his own offspring—try to kill their infant son by having him hobbled and exposed on Mount Cithaeron. The plot fails and the son grows up as the unknowing foster child of Polybus and Merope, the king and queen of Corinth. Reaching manhood, the son meets and kills a man on the road from Delphi to Thebes who is, unbeknown to him, his father. Then he proceeds to defeat the Sphinx and marry the queen, who is, again unbeknown to him, his mother. From this incestuous union are born four children—all doomed to die unhappy deaths—and eventually a lethal plague in Thebes, the cause of which the king is determined to eradicate.

The prominent features of each life are significant. In the first, intellect, energy, and fierce will combine to give Oedipus apparent control over his fate: he conquers the unruly Sphinx and (again, apparently) brings order and health to Thebes. By separating from his parents in Corinth and assuming command of a new environment, he creates himself as hero. The second, hidden life is ruled not by Oedipus's intellect or will but by mysterious divine forces that move inexorably beyond the reach of human control. Attempts by Jocasta and later by Oedipus to deny these forces their due are futile, as they both learn to their sorrow by play's end. The only comfort for one in grip of such forces is acceptance: as Paris puts it in the *Iliad*, the gifts of the gods are not to be refused (*Iliad* 3. 65–66). And in this version of himself, Oedipus, thinking to leave home and gain glory abroad, in fact returns home and does the one thing that always prevents the hero from achieving mature wisdom: he binds himself again to his own mother. In the heroic tradition, mothers are for unquestioning support; maturity and wisdom come from the father. Achilles must move beyond the sheltering of Thetis to the hard lessons learned from renewed contact with Priam, a surrogate for his father; and it is Anchises, not Venus, who shows Aeneas his duty in the underworld. The "detaining woman" in heroic stories, who threatens to keep the hero from his appointed tasks, carries the mother's resonance. Jocasta, as the wife of Oedipus, makes real what is in Circe or Dido only symbolic. At the same time, the oracle and Jocasta's response to it initially prevent the young Oedipus from reaching any kind of accommodation with his father. By later killing Laius, Oedipus cuts himself off completely and must find his own way.

Tiresias and the Life Cycle

These last relationships bring us back to issues of the life cycle. In the ancient hero's drive to separate from his mother and come to terms with his father, we see reflected the infant male's imperative to create himself by growing away from his mother and into the culture that reflects his father's public milieu—a movement, as we have seen, that is replayed in our time for men in early adulthood. The exchange between Oedipus and Tiresias represents symbolically the modern young man confronting parts of himself that had to be denied or pushed down below the level of conscious attention in order that the heroic Dream be born. As Levinson and his colleagues have shown (71–111; 139–165), the Dream is characteristically formed in the wake of the transition from late adolescence to early adulthood, and though it may be revised around age thirty in the light of experience, or even in some cases abandoned in favor of a new vision, it is much more common for this paradigm of the "good life" to rule until around age forty, when another major transition occurs.

But until each of us is ready to know what our version of Tiresias is telling us, we, like Oedipus, deny any kinship with other parts of ourselves that do not fit the Dream. The tenacity of our blindness is often stunning after the fact: *why* couldn't I see the truth? The answer to this question surely lies in the tight integration, in the heroic perspective, of our identity with our ability to work our will in the world. The traits that we stumble over in midlife and struggle to acknowledge in ourselves are precisely those not under our control—the inconvenient facts of biology that may impose limits on our will and thus on our self-creation. Because we can understand ourselves as the products of our will, the people we meet when Tiresias holds up the mirror are just not "us."

Viewed in this perspective, certain aspects of the exchange between Oedipus and the old prophet that seem to strain naturalism make more sense. Tiresias's reluctance to reveal what he knows, which comes as a surprise within the immediate context of events (and contrasts strongly with his eagerness in *Antigone*), is easier to grasp as a recognition that Oedipus is simply not ready to learn what he has to teach. Likewise, Oedipus's total inability even to entertain what Tiresias says about him, despite the tantalizing coincidence of his killing a stranger at the very time and place that Laius is said to have been murdered, challenges our credulity less if we see it as the behavior of a man in the grip of a powerfully distorting vision of who he is. Tiresias shows to Oedipus a version of himself that he has been denied by virtue of divine will, a force beyond the reach of his controlling intellect. To him, as to us when we see aspects of ourselves outside the Dream, the person looks like a stranger.

To say that we and Oedipus are "blind" to what falls outside the scope of our self-conception is to use a familiar metaphor. As it happens, the figure is especially potent in the context of this play, because Sophocles weaves his plot around the polarities of blindness/sight and ignorance/knowledge. We presuppose a correlation between the pairs, linking blindness with ignorance, knowledge with sight, and our assumptions have roots in the Greek language, where the same verb can mean visual perception and cognition. Our expectations prime us for Sophocles' ironies: Oedipus, the active, probing, keen-sighted intellectual "naturally" seems at first to have a more likely claim on the truth than a passive, blind old man. But in the course of the play, after fear and denial have their turn, what appears to be knowledge will finally prove to be ignorance, and from blindness will come the inner light of a more profound way of seeing.

Hunting the Shadow

A second major choral song follows Tiresias's exit. The anxiety we witnessed in the first song continues here, as the men wrestle with the issues raised by the quarrel between Oedipus and Tiresias. Who is the murderer? Can the prophet's charges against their king be true? Zeus and Apollo know the "dark and depth of human life," but the king has a spotless reputation, and they will wait for more proof before condemning him (463–511). Though the identity of the chorus in Greek tragedy varies widely, its voice in the plays of Sophocles that survive is usually communal, often representing, directly or indirectly, the values of the Athenian city state of the fifth century as a foil for the more archaic, problematic individualism of the hero. So here, the chorus weighs carefully the implications of the quarrel for the community: to offend the gods through their prophet is dangerous, but the king guides the city, and is its most immediate symbol of right order. In their conventional piety, these men would assume that civic order should ultimately reflect divine order, so the quarrel represents a serious dilemma for them, as at once citizens subject to the authority of Oedipus and mortals under the rule of the gods. The potential conflict between the hero and his community now grows more real in Thebes: as Oedipus draws nearer to the truth of his identity, the dishar-

mony within him is reflected outwardly in the increasing strain
on the chorus to support their king and stay true to the gods.

Creon now enters the scene, having heard that Oedipus has
been attacking him. The chorus are cautiously vague in reply to
his questions, but soon Oedipus arrives and leaves nothing in
doubt: Creon is a traitor, having conspired with Tiresias to overthrow the king and grab power for himself. Themes from
Antigone continue in the ensuing exchange, as each man accuses
the other of undervaluing kinship in pursuit of power: How
could Creon attack me, Oedipus, his own kin? Why would I,
Creon, attack my own kin, when the ties of blood ensure my status? The portrait of Creon is, in fact, somewhat ironic against
the background of the earlier work. Railing against Antigone
and his own son in the first play, Creon is obsessed with guarding every scrap of leverage the kingship gives him against the
claims of kinship forwarded by both. Here, his defense against
the charge of conspiracy is that he has no need of the responsibilities of kingship, since as a blood relative of the queen he already enjoys the power that being in the ruling family brings:
why ask for all those headaches when he already has the perks
(583–615)?

As he did with Tiresias, so here Oedipus lashes out at someone else, rather than consider whether what the prophet said
about him might be true. Sophocles' ironies flourish in Oedipus's ignorance, as he flails at yet another surrogate for himself.
From our perspective, the scene dramatizes the continued operation of denial in the hero, with its accompanying anger and
projection. On this level, too, there is irony:

OEDIPUS:

You—here? You have the gall
to show your face before the palace gates?

You, plotting to kill me, kill the king—
I see it all, the marauding thief himself
scheming to steal my crown and power!

(532–535)

The king is being killed, but not by Creon. Pushing ever closer to the facts of his birth, Oedipus drags his own heroic persona closer to the edge of destruction. There is a "conspiracy" of sorts involving Apollo's prophet, and Creon will succeed Oedipus as king in Thebes, but the co-conspirator is Oedipus, whose relentless heroic will drives him to expose his own buried life.

The Hero and His Mother

The exchange between Oedipus and Creon eventually becomes a shouting match, and Jocasta appears to see what all the commotion is about. Her response to what she finds reinforces the sense that there is something faintly *adolescent* about the two combatants:

Have you no sense? Poor misguided men,
such shouting—why this public outburst?
Aren't you ashamed, with the land so sick,
to stir up private quarrels?
                    (To Oedipus)
Into the palace now. And Creon, you go home.
Why make such a furor over nothing?

(634–639)

The orders go unheeded and the insults continue, punctuated by Jocasta's attempts to calm the men down and the chorus's anxious pleas for peace. Finally, Creon leaves, proclaiming his righteousness over his shoulder to an unrepentant Oedipus.

That Jocasta should make her initial appearance in the play at this juncture is telling. By having the two men quarrel like teenage siblings, Sophocles can bring out in Jocasta a distinctly maternal response. This role has no lasting resonance in her relationship with Creon, but of course it takes us directly into the darkest recesses of Oedipus's hidden life. Up to this point, the plot has focused our attention on the other half of the prophecy about Oedipus, the killing of Laius, but from now on the horror of incest also hovers over every scene.

Because incest, and especially incest with issue, scrambles fundamental boundaries of identity, this part of Oedipus's misperceived past life intensifies our awareness of the cost, to all of his family, of his ignorance. On the naturalistic level, our response, like those of the characters onstage, is likely one of revulsion: Sophocles' realization of the hero's life powerfully dramatizes the connection between biology and identity, pressing its implications with vivid impact. Moving back a step, we can look at Oedipus's incest in a way that recaptures its relevance in a wider context. Mothers in the heroic tradition are associated like all Greek women in antiquity with the private life of the family, in contrast to the masculine public arena. In the hero's imperative to leave the orbit of his mother and enter his father's world, we see reflected the need for the young Greek male to move beyond the private, sheltering, but restrictive embrace of his family into public life. The importance of this shift is not primarily geographical: Greek males often remained in the household of their birth after they reached adulthood. Rather, the significance of the separation from childhood is emotional. The young man must separate emotionally from the world of his childhood and the identity it provided; he must become self-reliant through acting out into the world, able to take responsibility for himself and eventually for his aged parents. For our purposes, the significance of this move is in the change in the male's location within the polarity nature/culture. Moving from private to public life entails, as we have seen, a shift in the basis of identity—from the facts of biology to actions taken in the context of human culture. To put it another way, the young man moves from being a part of nature to being a manipulator of nature—from created to creator.

All of this is well within the experience of modern men in pursuit of the Dream. The analogy to Oedipus's incest here would be a failure fully to embrace the new, self-created heroic persona, and the accompanying responsibilities that go, in this model of maturing, with adulthood. It is important to emphasize that we are not talking here about those men who, for reasons beyond the scope of our discussion, never start after the Dream in the first place. Sophocles' Oedipus plays help to illuminate the implications of having made that choice, not why one person does and another does not. Oedipus has already begun his heroic career when he returns to Thebes and claims his bride, and the analogy for our time might be expressed as a failure to follow through in grasping the promise that the self-created life offers; it is not in declining the heroic self in the first place.

We should also observe that the role of *conscious choice* in the shaping of the heroic life is not clear. If the dynamic of identity formation in infancy is replayed for males in late adolescence, then we can say that the imperatives of the Dream may well exert their power below the level of conscious choice. And we may add to this the incessant messages sent by our culture about how to achieve success and happiness, which are themselves active prior to conscious choice. My experience with young men (including myself), for what it is worth, convinces me that the urge to pursue the heroic Dream is usually felt deeply and often unreflectively: this is what you *do*, and this is who you *are*, when you grow up. That the resulting myopia brings pain as well as rewards is not so obvious.

Conclusion: Innocence and Guilt

It is true to Sophocles' ironic vision that, in trying to separate from his parents, Oedipus binds himself to them in a ruinous way. Because of his fundamental ignorance about his origins, everything that Oedipus does has a doubleness: all of his decisions, taken with the right motives (i.e., sanctioned by the heroic perspective), turn back on him and produce the wrong results. It is common to talk of the innocence or guilt of Oedipus, and from a legal or moral standpoint this is appropriate: ignorance does not always excuse wrongdoing. In this regard, it has seemed important to many students of the play to make a distinction between what Oedipus did before the play opens, killing his father and marrying his mother, and what he does in response to the immediate crisis of the plague. In the former case, the role of divine will seems more prominent, and Oedipus can be understood as the victim of outside forces beyond his control (though the killing of Laius shows us a rather rash, impetuous response to a seemingly mild affront). In the latter arena, Oedipus's acts might seem more his own—more the result of conscious choices not affected so directly by divine will, or "fate," and so presenting a less cloudy moral picture.

From our perspective this set of distinctions is less central, because our attention is focused elsewhere, not so much on the moral implications, for himself and for the community, of *what* Oedipus does, as on *how* ignorance about certain facts of his makeup lead him to act, with the best of intentions, in a destructive and self-destructive way. And because Oedipus's original misperceptions are fundamental to his later identity, out of which he acts in response to the plague, the distinction between past and present acts is less important. Likewise, the story teaches us about ourselves because the ignorance of Oedipus, enforced in the play by divine will and the response of Laius and Jocasta to it, symbolizes for us a selective blindness that can, it seems, be built into our postadolescent understanding of who we are and who we are to become. This narrow focus does not excuse us from responsibility for acts we may commit under its influence, but understanding the nature of our blindness in pursuit of the Dream can help us to accept the new parts of ourselves that we eventually confront, later in life.

2

SELF-DESTRUCTION
AS SELF-CREATION

Oedipus Rex 2

No one can be moral—that is, no one can harmonize con-
tained conflicts—without coming to a working arrange-
ment between the angel in himself and the devil in himself,
between his rose above and his manure below.

Alan Watts, *The Book*

The entrance of Jocasta marks a shift in focus of the play. Up to
this point, the plot has been pushed along by Oedipus's initiative in the present, generating the ironic doubleness we have observed in his actions and their consequences. Following the im
peratives of his heroic will to act as a way of controlling the
world and its problems, Oedipus has launched an investigation,
producing surprising and upsetting results, but he has managed
to escape facing the consequences of the exchange with Tiresias.
After Creon leaves the stage, our attention is drawn back in-
creasingly to the past, as the events surrounding Oedipus's birth
and exposure on Mount Cithaeron inexorably come to light.
The revelations, as always in the play, are finally forced into the
open by Oedipus's driving will. But the heroic determination is
redirected now, away from saving Thebes—we hear no more of
the plague—and toward solving the question of the king's true
identity. Yet even if Oedipus's attention is diverted from his civic
duties, the projection of his inner state out onto the civic order

continues. As Oedipus's heroic persona slowly collapses under the weight of the revelations, the health of the city begins to seem imperiled: if Oedipus is not who he thought he was, then the stability of the order he represents is also in question. And as the king is driven to adopt ever more desperate explanations to escape the realities of his past, the problematic nature of the relation between the hero and his community surfaces again. The plague, which began as a problem outside of Oedipus, has become a problem *about* him, and as he reluctantly turns inward to face his illness, the city's original affiliation with him looks more and more like a Faustian bargain.

Prophecy Under Attack

Characteristically, the final destruction of Oedipus's heroic persona begins with Jocasta's attempt to shore it up. He has told her that he suspects collusion between Creon and "his" prophet, Tiresias, and of the frightening charge that Tiresias has made against him. Her response is immediate and firm:

> A prophet?
> Well then, free yourself of every charge!
> Listen to me and learn some peace of mind:
> no skill in the world,
> nothing human can penetrate the future.
> Here is proof, quick and to the point.
>
> (707–710)

She goes on to recount the prophecy that Laius would be killed by his offspring, the exposure of their only son on Mount Cithaeron, and the subsequent killing of Laius by "thieves" at the crossroads. The prophecies, she concludes, were wrong, and so the prophets cannot claim to know the future. She ends with what for the audience is an ominous assertion:

Whatever the god needs and seeks
he'll bring to light himself, with ease.

(724–725)

The process has been underway since the play's first scene.

Oedipus is not reassured; rather, his thoughts begin to race. *Where* was Laius killed? *When?* As Jocasta replies, the pace of his self-discovery quickens: he remembers that *he* killed several men, and just at the time Laius is said to have died. More details come out, and his dread grows. He tells Jocasta the story of his youthful decision to leave Corinth to check the truth of a drunkard's claim that he did not know his own parents, of the horrifying prophecy that he would kill his father and marry his mother, of his encounter with an older man and his entourage at the same crossroads, how he killed them all in anger because they would not let him pass (771–813). If this man was Laius, then Oedipus has cursed *himself*, doomed *himself* to exile or death. He would rather disappear from the world of mortals, become *aphantos* (invisible) than to see himself "stained with such corruption" (831–833). The role of doctor that Oedipus assumed at the beginning of the play is now becoming untenable for him: he may instead be, as Tiresias claimed, the corruption that infects Thebes.

There is one last hope. One man escaped from the crossroads and returned to tell the Thebans what happened. When he saw Oedipus on the throne, he begged to be sent off into the wilderness as a shepherd. Oedipus seizes on a slender chance for escape: the man said "thieves" had attacked Laius, and Oedipus acted alone; let the shepherd be brought to confirm his story. Jo-casta insists that he did say "thieves," and reminds Oedipus that, in any event, prophecies are unreliable; Laius was not killed by his son: "So much for prophecy. It's neither here nor there" (857–858).

There is much here that strains the bounds of naturalism. Can it be that Oedipus was never struck by the coincidence be-tween his trouble on the road and the murder of Laius? Would he never have told his wife about the incident? Or about his childhood? These are valid issues, and they are not resolved in the play. Here again, however, there are other ways to under-stand the import of what some have considered lapses. First, we might reply that, from a dramatic standpoint, the revelation of this material here has a powerful impact. One of the most ad-mired aspects of Sophocles' technique in *Oedipus Rex* is the way the hero's *anagnoresis* (recognition) and his *peripeteia* (reversal of fortune) occur simultaneously: *when* something is revealed is as important in this context as *what* is learned. And from the psy-chological perspective we have been developing, Oedipus's ob-tuseness is of a piece with his earlier response to Tiresias: that he only begins to put the pieces of the story together after being bombarded with evidence incriminating him emphasizes the power of denial in the hero, driven by his powerful will, fueled by his distorted idea of who he is. The events in the outer life of Oedipus, revealed as they are here, do not always withstand scrutiny; as a picture of the inner evolution of the hero toward a truer portrait of his basic identity, the story is powerful and accurate.

Jocasta's fierce insistence on Oedipus's innocence also has a multiple resonance. As his wife and queen, she obviously has an investment in preserving his heroic persona. But we have seen that Sophocles also emphasizes her maternal bond to Oedipus—a role that has portentous implications for him as a hero and as a man. We have said that ancient heroes look to their mothers for unquestioning support, to their fathers for wisdom—the latter often harsh and difficult to accept. Until she is forced by Zeus's intervention to urge Achilles toward the new perspective that allows him to release the body of Hector, Thetis consistently supports her son in behavior that is self-destructive. Gilgamesh's mother endorses wholeheartedly his journey to the Cedar Forest to kill the monster Humbaba, an act of hubris that will cost him his friend Enkidu. Venus, the mother of Aeneas, arranges for his tryst with Dido in Carthage, deflecting him from the role Jupiter has assigned him, then abets the destruction of the union before Aeneas can learn anything from it. As Oedipus draws nearer to the truth about his past, Jocasta tries ever more desperately to block his access to self-knowledge. Thinking that the old shepherd will clear Oedipus in the search for Laius's killer, she reassures him as they leave the stage:

I'll send at once. But do let's go inside.
I'd never displease you, least of all in this.

(861–862)

The Child of Chance
The choral song that follows reflects the increasing strain on the community of Oedipus's struggle. And as the truth crashes down on the king, the collapse of his world seems to send out ripples that reach even beyond the confines of the city. The chorus begin by reaffirming their reverence for the eternal laws given to mortals by the gods, then move to condemn the pride of overbearing tyrants, which threatens the order sanctioned by those laws. How this portrait relates to Oedipus is left unclear:

it *could* refer only to the unknown murderer of Laius. In the final stanza, the ambiguity grows more acute:

Never again will I go reverent to Delphi,
    the inviolate heart of the Earth
or Apollo's ancient oracle at Abae
or Olympia of the fires—
    unless these prophecies all come true
for all mankind to point toward in wonder.
King of kings, you deserve your titles
    Zeus, remember, never forget!
You and your deathless, everlasting reign.

They are dying, the old oracles sent to Laius,
now our masters strike them off the rolls.
    Nowhere Apollo's golden glory now—
        the gods, the gods go down.

(897–910)

The radical doubt about Oedipus's origins and identity has cosmic implications that are mirrored in the chorus's anxious attempts to make sense of the world: if prophecies cannot be trusted, then neither can the gods; if the gods are not to be trusted, then where do we look for assurance that the world makes sense? From the opening scene of the play, Oedipus has presented himself as the gods' agent, the mortal guarantor of order in the city. Now his crumbling heroic persona threatens to take Thebes down with it. The heroic bringer of order is becoming an agent of chaos.

Jocasta reappears, carrying the branch of a suppliant. She approaches the altars in front of the palace—which, we finally learn, are Apollo's—and prays to the god to set the Thebans free of defilement. We have returned to the play's opening scene, but Oedipus can no longer stand in for Apollo. He is, Jocasta tells us, wracked with fear and doubt. The circular structure underscores how much has changed—how thoroughly the heroic confidence of the king has been undermined. A messenger enters, innocently eager to deliver the news that will launch Oedipus's final descent from tyrant to criminal, from hero to polluted outcast. There is no ancient drama with a tighter structure and more effective plot than *Oedipus Rex*, and the next scene is the masterpiece of the play. Modulating the dialogue with a faultless ear, Sophocles puts us on the rack with Oedipus, drawing out the execution. As the truth comes forward, every attempt to deflect it only adds to its force; each revelation, delivered in hopes of freeing Oedipus, pushes him closer to the brink of an abyss that appears, in the play's tragic perspective, to be bottomless.

The messenger is from Corinth. The old king has died, and Oedipus is called to be king. Jocasta, delighted with this further evidence that the prophecies were wrong, sends for Oedipus. The king arrives immediately, and hearing the news, questions the old man carefully: Was it murder? A natural death? Sickness took him off, it seems, and now Oedipus joins Jocasta in dismissing the prophecies as worthless. The euphoria is short-lived, however: what about the queen? Oedipus must remain vigilant while she lives, in fear of fulfilling the other part of the prophecy. Jocasta impatiently dismisses his qualm:

> Fear?
> What should a man fear? It's all chance,
> chance rules our lives. Not a man on earth
> can see a day ahead, groping through the dark.
> Better to live at random, best we can.
> And as for this marriage with your mother—

have no fear. Many a man before you,
in his dreams, has shared his mother's bed.
Take such things for shadows, nothing at all—
Live, Oedipus,
as if there's no tomorrow!

(977–983)

These lines, so compelling centuries later to Freud, may be the most famous in the play. But from our perspective, it is not the evidence of the "Oedipus complex" that draws attention. More telling is the enthroning of chance. All through the play, we have seen that there is an intimate connection between Oedipus's inner life and the health of the city. On a political level, within the frame of the story, the citizens view their ruler as the symbol of right order sanctioned by the larger divine order; from our perspective as spectators outside the story, the linkage appears as a dramatic, mimetic device, objectifying in the city the subjective state of Oedipus. In the context of these correspondences, Jocasta's speech becomes part of the movement from order to chaos, inside the hero, outside in the city and beyond to the very structure of the cosmos. We have seen that the Greeks of Sophocles' time thought of Chance as a deity, and that she was usually imagined as embodying an element of randomness within the larger order of the gods. Jocasta's speech suggests another, more troubling interpretation that only became common in Greek thought a century or so later: Chance, she seems to be saying, exists outside of the order sanctioned by the other gods. The queen, buoyed by the latest news, sees no evidence that the divine order can be seen to function on the human level: all is decided at random; the world cannot be understood, so why try? Instead, live for the moment; do not look for guidance in a larger order.

In Jocasta's words we recognize a crisp summary of what we call an existentialist view of the world: we ask the world to explain itself, and it declines—it is "absurd." (The Latin root here is related to the word for deafness—the world cannot hear us.) In the moral uncertainty of mid-twentieth-century Europe, this view was compelling: if God is dead, then we must create our own meaning through *action*; no higher order guarantees meaning; existence precedes essence. The heroic resonance of this view is also clear: Camus' Dr. Rieux, fighting the plague without hope, is an essentially Homeric character. The chorus's fears have come true. Discarding prophecy, the king and queen have thrown away the divine order that guarantees meaning on earth. Jocasta now goes a step further: if Chance is truly an independent force, then nothing makes sense: to live at random in the religious and moral world of Periclean Athens is to plunge into frightening chaos.

Oedipus remains wary, and the messenger politely asks why. Oedipus reveals the old prophecy, and the man cheerfully—and at excruciating leisure—tells him not to worry: *they* were not his real parents; he was an orphan, given as an infant to the messenger himself; see, his ankles still bear the marks of the piercing for which he was named. But who was the man who gave the infant away? One of Laius's men, he thinks. We imagine Jocasta stiffening here: for her, the denial is over. But Oedipus has a moment or two left to dream. Pressed for the identity of Laius's servant, the Corinthian suspects it may be the very shepherd that Oedipus has already summoned, but he defers to Jocasta for certainty. Now begins the final exchange between the king and his queen, Oedipus pushing characteristically to *know* everything, Jocasta begging him to stop the search. He mistakes her reluctance for snobbery: she would not want a foundling, maybe a slave, for her consort. She finally runs into the palace, having

pronounced him doomed: May he never know who he is! (1069).
Self-knowledge is the wisdom to be gained by this hero, at whatever cost, and his mother, true to her traditional role, cannot finally help him.

Oedipus's denial swells to one last crescendo:

Let it burst! Whatever will, whatever must!
I must know my birth, no matter how common
it may be—I must see my origins face-to-face.
She perhaps, with her woman's pride
may well be mortified by my birth,
but I, I count myself the son of Chance,
the great goddess, giver of all good things—
I'll never see myself disgraced. She is my mother!
And the moons have marked me out, my blood-brothers,
one moon on the wane, the next moon great with power.
That is my blood, my nature—I will never betray it,
never fail to search and learn my birth!

(1076–1085)

The old fire is back, and with it much of the heroic myopia
we have seen all through the play. This narrowed vision leads
him into a contradictory, and finally untenable, position. Once
again, Oedipus sees himself linked to the gods—this time by
birth—and he uses this link to push against the restraints of
human life. As with Achilles, his semidivine status makes him
defy ordinary limits; the true facts of his birth, which have lately
seemed able to threaten his heroic autonomy, will finally, as he
sees it, free him. And this particular genealogy seems to extend
his autonomy even further. Following Jocasta's lead, he embraces
Chance as his patron deity, and so imagines himself able—true
to his heroic perspective—to step outside even the constraints

of divine will, to live at random. Like his divine mother, he exists outside the cosmic plan guaranteed by other deities; his heroic self-inflation has carried him beyond all limit now.

But of course his origins are other than he imagines, and tracking them down will have the opposite effect from what he imagines in his heroic fantasy. The great, restless energy continues trained with fierce intensity on a mystery, one that he sees as different from the earlier problem of the plague. But we know that the mystery has always been the same, and his defiant words come to our ears filtered through Sophocles' relentless irony. The heroic desire to *know*, to control disorder through imposing structure on what looks like chaos, has brought Oedipus to an inescapable impasse: the object of his knowing, once grasped, will drain the strength from his grip. Blood and moons are the province of women in the Greek imagination. To glory in his bonds to these powers is for Oedipus to place himself beyond the reach of heroic self-assertion—to reenter the constraining and defining boundaries of his biology, the very place he has been running from.

The chorus catch the spirit of Oedipus's last gambit and respond with a short burst of lyrical optimism. Oedipus is, after all, the son of deities. Is Apollo his father? Hermes? Dionysus? Is his mother a numinous mountain nymph? Notice that the chorus do not endorse Chance as a worthy parent: the stakes are too high for the community if the king embodies the spirit of randomness. But the city's health remains, in the eyes of these citizens, linked firmly to the fortunes of its ruler.

The Death of the Dream

Jocasta has gone; Oedipus, the Corinthian messenger, and the chorus remain onstage. The king catches sight of an old man walking toward him:

I never met the man, my friends . . . still,
if I had to guess, I'd say that's the shepherd,
the very one we've been looking for all along.
Brothers in old age, two of a kind,
he and our guest here. At any rate
the ones who bring him in are my own men,
I recognize them.

(1110–1115)

Here is another brilliant piece of theater. As the old shepherd creeps reluctantly along, goaded by Oedipus's guards, he approaches the king across a relatively short dramatic space in the theater. To *us* he shambles forward from a vast distance, across time from that day when the royal couple gave him their infant to expose on Mount Cithaeron. We know, and every audience before us has known, what he brings: he is indeed the one Oedipus has been looking for all along. After the old man finally arrives center stage (if I were directing, this would take a while), Sophocles draws out the revelation of Oedipus's identity for another seventy-five lines, the shepherd evading, the Corinthian messenger helpfully prompting, and Oedipus, as always, prodding. Finally, Oedipus grasps the whole truth:

O god—
All come true, all burst to light!
O light—now let me look my last on you!
I stand revealed at last—
cursed in my birth, cursed in marriage,
cursed in the lives I cut down with these hands!

(1182–1185)

These are Oedipus's last words as traditional hero, and he rushes offstage. When he returns in this play, blind and bleeding, he is already changed, has already begun the next stage in his long life-journey toward that grand and mysterious exit from this world in Sophocles' last work.

The Dream has died, and it is fitting that an old man should be its final executioner. The shepherd is, in fact, the third old man to bring Oedipus news of his real identity, and he tells us nothing essential about Oedipus that was not delivered by the first one, Tiresias, and confirmed by his "brother in old age," the Corinthian messenger: the three are, we might say, "triples" of each other. The function of this repeated "type" within the story may be understood in at least two ways. Insofar as the messenger and the shepherd carry on the work of Tiresias in particular, they become aged midwives for the other Oedipus who has been lost all those years: the other Oedipus has been walking toward the king of Thebes since he left Corinth. At the same time, seen within in the framework of the hero story as symbolic representation of the hero's maturation, the figure of the old man fills the place of the father, as Priam does for Achilles. Priam's plea for the release of his son Hector's body, which prompts the speech about the two jars of Zeus and the unity of all mortals, begins with the words "remember your father" (*Iliad* 24. 486). Like the old men in *Oedipus Rex*, Priam takes the role of Achilles' father in leading him toward wisdom, and in the old shepherd's slow walk across the stage we can see a reflection of Priam's lonely trek across the plain of Troy toward Achilles' hut. Oedipus has been offered three chances to grasp the hard wisdom about himself and, by extension, the meaning of his life, that the hero's *father* ordinarily delivers. To accept it at last is, in the terms of the ancient narrative, to move into a new stage in life, out of the self-created heroic fantasy, supported by his mother, and into a more complex world governed by transcendent forces beyond human control. This postheroic world is what we will see through the blinded eyes of the aged Oedipus.

Rushing off stage in his pain, Oedipus is carried by the last ebbing of a titanic wave of energy that has driven the play from its opening scene. Gone with him are the Corinthian heroic persona he has nurtured and defended and the whole structure of his world as he has come to know it. Looking to create and confirm meaning in his life, Oedipus has destroyed the basis for that meaning and has left chaos in its place. It is the chorus, as usual, who voice the fear in the hero's wake:

> O the generations of men
> the dying generations—adding the total
> of all your lives I find they come to nothing . . .
>   does there exist, is there a man on earth
> who seizes more joy than just a dream, a vision?
> And the vision no sooner dawns than dies
> blazing into oblivion.
>
> You are my great example, you, your life
> your destiny, Oedipus, man of misery—
> I count no man blest.
>
>   (1186–1195)

The hero is the *paradeigma* (the model); taking his measure, the chorus can only conclude that human life is finally *meden* (nothing). Reviewing his rise to heroic splendor and later fall into horror brings these ordinary citizens to see their original bargain with the wondrous stranger in a somber light:

>   But now for all your power
> Time, all-seeing Time has dragged you to the light,
> judged your marriage monstrous from the start—
> the son and father tangling, both one—

O child of Laius, would to god
  I'd never seen you, never never!
  Now I weep like a man who wails the dead
and the dirge comes pouring forth from my heart!
I tell you the truth, you gave me life
my breath leapt up in you
and now you bring down night upon my eyes.

(1213–1221)

Oedipus, like all heroes, offers at first an escape from time—a vision of life that defies limits—but finally his surge toward godhead comes full circle and leads to the definitive human characteristic, death.

True to the rich layering of meanings in the play, the universal imperative of mortality for humans has already found its paradigm on stage, in the death of the heroic, Corinthian Oedipus. In his last words before leaving, this man marks his own passing as dying heroes often do, saluting the light for the last time:

             O god—
all come true, all burst to light!
O light—now let me look my last on you!
I stand revealed at last—
cursed in my own birth, cursed in marriage,
cursed in the lives I cut down with these hands!

(1182–1185)

It is characteristic of Sophocles' vision that for Oedipus the finding of his true self demands the death of his heroic persona. But the playwright is not done with his creation yet. In the last scenes of the play, the acts of Oedipus point, however tentatively, beyond the seeming cul-de-sac of the heroic life, as he gropes to-

ward some new way of understanding the world and his place in
it. Traveling with him, we are offered a glimpse at the first stage
of life, for Oedipus and for us, beyond heroism. The journey begins with self-mutilation.

Self-Blinding as Punishment

As the chorus's song dies away, a messenger arrives. The
Athenian audience, if they are regular theatergoers, know what
kind of news to expect. Greek tragic drama never enacts physical violence in open view; rather, the deeds are done offstage, and
then reported. So here, we learn of Jocasta's suicide by hanging,
and then of Oedipus's response:

He rips off her brooches, the long gold pins
holding her robes—and lifting them high,
looking straight up into the points,
he digs them down the sockets of his eyes, crying, "You,
you'll see no more the pain I suffered, all the pain I caused!
Too long you looked on the ones you never should have seen,
blind to ones you longed to see, to know! Blind
from this hour on! Blind in the darkness—blind!"

(1268–1274)

The intricate layers of imagery organized throughout the
play around the polarities of light/dark, knowledge/ignorance
come to fruition in this potent act. And as Oedipus's *last* major
act in the play, it cannot fail to be definitive. Now, apparently re-
pulsed by the evidence of his misguided actions, he shuts out the
light. Following the usual associations of light in Greek culture
and our own, we are likely to understand this as a drastic *punishment*: no more access to the medium of independence, happiness, growth, knowledge; into the world of sadness, death, ignorance, dependence. Certainly this is how the chorus see it: "I

shudder at the sight" (1306); "Dreadful what you've done . . . /
how could you bear it, gouging out your eyes?" (1327–1328).
Those modern commentators pursuing a Freudian interpretation see the self-mutilation as a punishment for incest; they cite
other instances in Greek literature where those who transgress,
especially in some sexual way, are blinded, and go from there to
self-blinding as a symbolic castration.

Tiresias exemplifies a telling qualification: those who act
wrongly but *unintentionally* are often compensated for the loss of
eyesight by increased *insight*, usually in the form of prophetic wisdom. Such stories reflect a belief—in ancient and modern cultures—that those without eyesight are somehow more attuned
to other forms of knowledge than the sighted: Homer's blindness helps to explain his extraordinary insight into human nature; more mundanely, we believe now that the other senses—
touch, taste, smell, hearing—are especially acute in blind
people.

Oedipus, ignorant of his real identity, would seem to fit into
this latter category of unintentional wrongdoers. But his case is
unusual, we might say, because he blinds *himself*. Indeed, he insists
on his own agency in the act itself:

> Apollo, friends, Apollo—
> he ordained my agonies—these, my pains on pains!
> But the hand that struck my eyes was mine,
> mine alone—no one else—
> I did it myself!
> What good were eyes to me?
> Nothing I could see could bring me joy.
>
> (1329–1335)

Here we see vestiges of Oedipus's heroic will: he will judge
and punish himself, taking a role often reserved for gods. And

his understanding of the blinding and its justification suggests
no compensatory gain in insight:

What I did was best—don't lecture me,
no more advice. I, with *my* eyes,
how could I look my father in the eyes
when I go down to death? Or mother, so abused . . .
I have done such things to the two of them,
crimes too huge for hanging.
                    Worse yet,
the sight of my children, born as they were born,
how could I look into their eyes?
No, not with these eyes of mine, never.

                                     (1369–1377)

Austere, unrelenting, Oedipus speaks in the voice of the traditional, self-destructive hero who has transgressed and cannot
live with the shame invoked by his acts: Sophocles' Ajax is an apt
parallel, killing himself rather than live with the consequences of
a madness sent on him by Athena. There is no hint here of any
relief, of any hope for a new perspective in the darkness. Godlike, Oedipus has made himself by imposing his will on the
world; displeased with his creation, he destroys it. But we have
seen that Sophocles offers other modes of being in the world to
contrast with Oedipus, and in particular, Tiresias. Returning to
the complementary relationship between Oedipus and Tiresias
allows us a glimpse at what is to come for Oedipus.

Self-Blinding and the Hero's Death-Unto-Self

The intersection of Oedipus's movement into darkness with
the death of his heroic persona is, in itself, comfortably within
the bounds of the traditional hero story. The pattern of separa-

tion and return, at the core of many heroic narratives, takes the
hero out of his normal place and into some new arena, offering
knowledge and experience beyond the ordinary, where only one
with his special qualities can go. Once returned, he can share his
precious insight with those left behind. A trip to the underworld, where the hero looks death in the face and comes back to
tell of it, is the most vivid realization of this process. Such a
journey offers profound metaphors for the movement of the
hero toward spiritual wholeness: by entering the realm of the
dead, he puts himself at the mercy of the force that marks the
limits of human control, and so, by extension, imperils his very
identity as hero. Gilgamesh, seeking escape from his mortality
in the wake of Enkidu's death, travels to the Land of Dilmun,
across the Waters of Darkness. Utnapishtim, his surrogate father, offers deep, if unwelcome truth: all mortals must die. After
vain attempts to win a special dispensation, Gilgamesh finally
accepts his lot and returns to rule his city a wiser, more mature
man. Achilles makes the same kind of journey, but symbolically.
After Patroclus dies, grief drives Achilles into a spiritual darkness, a death-unto-self, from which he returns with a new perspective on his place in the world after accepting his mortality
at the urging of Priam, another surrogate father.

The modern metaphor for this darkness is the unconscious,
where the conscious ego is no longer in control—the repository
of aspects of the self that must finally be acknowledged if we are
to realize our full potential as humans: Jung's individuation begins, as we have said, with the acknowledgement of unconscious
elements of the self. In both the ancient and modern metaphors,
annihilation of the conscious, controlling self allows access to
deeper truths that in turn show the way to a new understanding
of one's self and place in the world; in both, it is the experience of
powerlessness that opens the way to a new kind of empowerment.

Oedipus, plunging into darkness by his own hand, realizes the death of his Corinthian persona in a characteristically rich way. The self-blinding, a renunciation of the agency through which he has been powerful and through which he has defined himself, is understood by all onstage to be a punishment—and so it is, if heroic agency is considered the ultimate good. But it is also analogous to the hero's voluntary trip to the underworld, where he risks being subject to the ultimate limit of human control—and thus a diminishing of agency—in search of knowledge unavailable to the ordinary person. The first meaning of the blinding is valid within the limited perspective of the old, Corinthian Oedipus; the second points beyond heroic self-assertion toward another way of seeing. We may begin to follow out the implications of this new vision by recognizing that—as modern students of the play have often noted—the blinding is a move *toward* the figure of Tiresias, the repository in this play of Oedipus's buried life. The old, heroic Oedipus must die before a new man can be born, and the key to this new man is to be found in what Tiresias reflects back to him.

Mortality marks the limit of heroic assertion. Tiresias offers this perspective to Oedipus, but indirectly, by implication. In his prophecies, he undermines the way Oedipus understands *why* he has become the man he thinks he is. The power to control the world, which had seemed the basis for Oedipus's identity and, by extension, for the meaning of his life, is shown to be an illusion. Instead, mysterious, transcendent forces have shaped his life in a way that neither he nor his parents could avoid. Oedipus denies these truths until, through the shepherd and the Corinthian messenger, the facts of Oedipus's birth—his place as a biological son in the larger structures of nature—come to light and confirm what Tiresias has said. The complexity of Sophocles' dramatic technique can at times be overwhelming

and may blur a point essential for our purposes: the world of nature, the gods, and fate—though the relations between them as
the Greeks understood them are often complicated—are all
analogous in one sense: that they finally transcend and limit
human control. And all confirm by this transcendence the basic
fact of mortality. Tiresias shows Oedipus his powerlessness in
the face of all three forces: the natural world, reflected in his biological links to Laius and Jocasta; his fate, as revealed in the
prophecies; the will of the gods, represented by Apollo's surrogate, the prophet.

By blinding himself, Oedipus can be understood to mark on
one level a belated *acceptance* of all that Tiresias showed him in
their encounter: the apparent powerlessness of the blind man
becomes an emblem for the essential place of humans *within* the
larger cosmos, rather than *outside* it, as agents. Showing us this
much, Sophocles traces a familiar journey in the hero narrative,
from solipsistic egotism to humility. This far many hero stories
take us, but no further; having brought the hero through the
death-unto-self to the threshold of a new perspective, the stories end. The tone of the response onstage to and by the blinded
Oedipus seems to leave us at best on that threshold. It will be another twenty years before Sophocles returns to the story, to take
Oedipus beyond traditional heroism. Meanwhile, we may pause
to consider the implications for the adult life cycle of what has
happened to Oedipus.

Death-Unto-Self Within the Life Cycle

Helpless and grotesque, the blind Oedipus appears to be at
the end of any meaningful life, as such a life is defined in the
heroic perspective. Cut off from the light, he cannot act out into
the world to create meaning: his agency has been extinguished.
As he is led off the stage at the end of the play by Creon, the fu-

ture is opaque at best. In the view of all onstage, the question of whether he ought to be exiled or killed, as his own command decreed, does not seem compelling; he is, after all, dead already in the ways that count in that world. But though we can learn from Oedipus, his world—the artistic construct of Sophocles' play—is not finally ours: what is final in the symbolic matrix of Oedipus's heroic life is only a transition in our evolving journey; what leads to unnatural horror in Thebes can be, in the symbolic analogue of our inner selves, quite "natural" at a certain time in our lives. Indeed, the action of the play represents a phase in the lives of many men that is fairly common, and not necessarily "bad": the drive to make and do is not in itself negative; the hero can do much good, for himself and the community. The trouble comes, as we have said, when he cannot move beyond the Dream, by coming to terms with what he has denied in himself, and then finding a place for these elements as part of his identity. We return for the moment to modern studies of the adult life cycle.

We have seen that the formation of the Dream by young men comes at the end of a transition from adolescence to adult life. We have also observed that time and circumstances, cultural and/or biological, conspire to urge a heroic perspective on those who seek the Dream: ties to larger structures, in society and nature, that help define the identity of children, are devalued as the seeker creates himself through acting out into the objectified world. The fictive story of Oedipus has shown us how this view of oneself implies a particular relationship between knowledge, will, and power: the more he imposes his will on the world, the more authentically "himself" he becomes; the more himself he becomes, the more his sense of agency tells him that the world has meaning. This configuration seems to serve those adopting it until, sometime in the late thirties, when experience begins to challenge its assumptions, and the young man enters another transition period.

Of transition periods in general, Levinson says (51):

The task of developmental transition is to terminate a time in one's life: to accept the losses the termination entails; to review and evaluate the past; to decide which aspects of the past to keep and which to reject; and to consider one's wishes and possibilities for the future. One is suspended between past and future, and struggling to overcome the gap that separates them. Much from the past must be given up—separated from, cut out of one's life, rejected in anger, renounced in sadness or grief. And there is much that can be used as a basis for the future. Changes must be attempted in both self and world.

During any such period, we suffer a kind of death—of our ideas about who we are and where we fit: our old self dies to make room for the new version. This is necessary because, as Levinson reminds us (61), we cannot live out all aspects of the self during any one period of our lives. Like Oedipus, we find that the model of self-in-the-world we adopted earlier no longer fits the experience of being in the world, and like him, we may seek darkness in some form to renew contact with parts of ourselves that we have lost track of or never knew.

This latter journey is especially true of the midlife transition, when neglected parts of the self begin to shoulder their way into view. In our rush to launch the Dream, we may well bury parts of ourselves that do not fit the heroic mold. But for us, as for Oedipus, a reckoning eventually comes. And as Oedipus teaches us, the collapse of the old self amid the clamoring of other voices can have consequences beyond personal identity. Because the meaning of life for heroes is a product of the impress of a cer-

tain model of the self on the world, the undermining of the
heroic self can result in the meaning being drained out of life—
the event we call a midlife crisis. The chorus's anxieties in the
face of Oedipus's collapsing identity reflect out onto the community the crisis of meaning inside the king: if prophecies do
not reveal the will of the gods, the world cannot be charted.

The Other Oedipus and Midlife Reassessments: Young/Old

Though the polarity death/rebirth can inform all transition
periods in adult life, the dynamic is especially pronounced in the
midlife transition, because this is the time in life when deterio-
rating physical capacity, the death of friends, perhaps of rela-
tives, all make the fact of one's own ultimate mortality seem inescapable: I am a creature whose life on earth is finite. I will die.
Such a realization begins the process of undermining the heroic
illusion of a life without limits, and its growing power inside us
urges reassessment of other assumptions that follow from the
heroic perspective. At the same time, the finite nature of our existence can suddenly heighten the urgency of this reassessment:
if I have only so much time, then what I choose and reject are
crucial; the road not taken begins to look out of reach forever.

Tiresias shows Oedipus the shadowy outlines of his other
self. After a period of denial, the hero accepts the existence of
this new/old self and—in our reading—blinds himself as a way
of turning inward toward the darkness inside himself, to face
those aspects of his identity that have been kept from his conscious attention. *Individuation* (to use Jung's word) entails major
shifts in our idea of who we are and, by extension, of what life
means: this is the precious knowledge we can bring back from the
underworld. To make these changes, we characteristically confront certain polarities that inform our existence and try to find
ways to resolve them in a way that makes a new self possible. Res-

olution does not mean making the oppositions go away by choosing one side over the other; the tensions will always be present. Rather, we must accommodate the tensions by somehow transcending them. In the active, conscious life of Oedipus, Sophocles shows us the parameters of the heroic perspective and what it implies about identity: the other, buried Oedipus is just as illuminating for what limits and finally transcends this kind of vision.

Levinson (191–244), synthesizing the work of many modern scholars, sees four polarities as crucial to the midlife transition: Young/Old, Destruction/Creation, Masculine/Feminine, Attachment/Separateness. (We will rename this last pair, to avoid confusion with another distinction we have been drawing: Engagement/Detachment.) The most fundamental of these polarities is the first, and this should not surprise us since it raises issues related to the passing of time—the measure of mortality. The hero exists, in his assumptions about his powers, outside time. Then death becomes real, and suddenly he is a creature bounded by the shape of an individual life. In our late thirties, the fact of death becomes real for us, and we are suddenly in the *middle* of something, looking both backward to our youth and forward to some time in the future when it will all end. We are no longer young but not yet old. Like Oedipus, we face a sudden awareness of limits on our existence and our control over the shape of our life; our body ages whether we like it or not; we are ruled by forces beyond our control.

The story of Oedipus reflects the polarity Young/Old in another, more striking, way. When we reach middle age, it is also often the time when those who have children see them beginning to go through teenage adolescence. As parents, we have a peculiar double perspective on our children's struggles to cope with their changing bodies and their first attempts to move away from the sheltering embrace of family toward adulthood. As adults, we may be detached from this turmoil, since we are in a different place in our lives. At the same time, as parents, we identify with our children, and relive our own struggles through them: maybe we can get it *right* this time. And of course we—with *our* changing bodies—are moving into our own period of transition, which will require analogous adjustments, letting go of old selves, accepting new ones. And as we move toward forty, our own parents may well be entering old age. This will mean another fundamental change: the people we looked to for nurturing, and from whom we tried to distance ourselves in order to feel autonomous, will soon perhaps become ours to care for. They will need us as we needed them, and so we may feel besieged on both sides. In any event, we are *between* two other dramatic transitions being made by those to whom we are bound by blood. Pulled by conflicting roles and generations, we are, as parents and children, caught in the tension that characterizes transition periods.

Oedipus, ignorant of his true past, living the heroic life, cannot see his true relationship to his parents or his children. Once made aware of his birth and biology, he must face the horrendously compromised relationship he bears to both. Father and brother, son and lover, he is trapped between two roles that are definitive for understanding one's place in the world. As we have seen, Sophocles' play presents as objective and concrete what we may understand as subjective and symbolic. The fact of incest on the Athenian stage can symbolize in our lives a tension between young and old: we are at once young enough to feel our children's pain and yet moving into a time when the struggles of our parents will be more analogous to our own.

Destruction/Creation

I am watching television. On the screen come pictures of some place distant from me, where there is civil war. I identify the "good" side, according to my political preferences and my ideas about moral behavior. Of the "bad" people, I say: "How can they *do* that to other people? They're behaving like animals, not human beings." This has been a recurring scene in my life. Entering college during the time of the Vietnam War, I have ample opportunity to react to gruesome pictures on the screen. Doing so affords pleasures: I can feel "committed" to my beliefs—the stronger my outrage, the purer my motives. I can also feel superior to the "other side" (here include my parents, who are not able to achieve my level of purity)—*I* could never do that. I am intelligent, enlightened. But one day, when I have reached the age of thirty-eight, the scene ends differently. I watch, I condemn, and then suddenly realize that, put in the same circumstances as the "bad" people, I could not guarantee that I would act differently.

What happened to me is apparently a common event for those entering middle age. It may be understood in various ways. From a position of "enlightenment," I have moved into the dark. That darkness is inside me, I realize, and the discovery is not initially pleasant: I have the same capacity for destruction within me as any other human being. All of this follows from the fact of mortality. As a creature who will die, I am akin to the "animals" I condemned; like any other part of nature, I can destroy other living things. None of this fits comfortably within the heroic self-concept. Heroes realize their true selves only insofar as they defy limits: *no death*; heroes create meaning by controlling the forces of nature, including animals: *I am not a part of nature; I stand apart from it, a steward.*

But if the fact of mortality reminds us of our links to the rest of the natural world, it also pushes us to recognize and explore what makes us unusual *within* the natural world. We have observed that, given the apparently unique self-consciousness of human beings, the fact of death creates a certain urgency in us. With only a finite time left on this earth, we must make the most of it, by doing great things—by leaving, perhaps, some legacy after we die. Here we encounter the other side of the polarity: creativity. Badgers, not burdened by the nagging certitude of their passing, feel no need to write books about Greek tragedy; humans, because we weigh our acts in the light of our extinction, labor to beat death: "I have erected a monument more lasting than bronze," says Horace of his poetry (*Odes* 3.30.1). Humans are special, in that only we can destroy not as a part of an instinctual need to survive but out of hatred and spite; and only we can reflect on our existence and create moral and aesthetic monuments to that reflection. Both traits follow from the condition of being human; to accept our human nature, we must accept the presence of both in ourselves.

Such acceptance is unavailable to the Corinthian Oedipus. As self-created hero, he can understand himself as reflecting only one side of the polarity. As king, parent, child, and husband, he creates: civic harmony, healthy children, doting parents, a loving wife. Comes the plague, and he is unable to see his part in the destruction, flailing out at others, the "bad" people who must be stopped; enter Tiresias, with the news that the king is the sickness; Oedipus denies, deflecting the disease back onto the prophet and then to Creon. When the final blow is struck by the old shepherd, the Theban Oedipus is reborn, embodying both sides of the polarity with a terrifying richness. *This* Oedipus is a killer, of his father, of those citizens who died in the plague, and, by his relentless search for control through knowledge, of his own heroic self; *this* Oedipus has brought pain, through his unwitting incest, to his mother, wife, and children; *this* Oedipus, seeking to impose order on his adopted city, fosters chaos and fear.

Here again, Sophocles' powerful realization of the passage from Corinthian to Theban Oedipus, with its frightening and repugnant consequences in the naturalistic world of the play, may obscure its relevance for our lives. But Oedipus is *innocent*, we say; he is not responsible for the patricide and the incest. So he is, and yet in Sophocles' symbolic system, his ignorance becomes part of a blindness to his true self that follows from his heroic self-assertion. What Tiresias shows the king, in essence, is evidence of his humanness, embedded in, and defined by, his place in the larger order of the cosmos. Oedipus becomes the agent of destruction when he reenters the world of mortals from the godlike potency of the heroic perspective; in other words, that he cannot *help* destroying becomes, in the structure of the play, a condition of his humanity. And here is where we come in: like Oedipus, we may have lost track of our place in the scheme of things as we pursued the Dream; death becomes real for us, and we reenter the world of fallible mortals, where destruction is the other side of creation.

This is not to say that as humans we are doomed to do evil, but only that as a condition of our humanity we have the capacity for destruction; that to suppose we can embody only one side of the polarity is to claim that we can stand outside of the world that defines us. Once we leave the heroic perspective, that claim is no longer valid. All of this necessarily alters the context within which we make moral choices. In the heroic perspective, it is possible— indeed obligatory—to define oneself as embodying one side of the polarities: young, creative, masculine, engaged. The dark parts of human existence are projected "out there," onto an objectified world on which we act. Thus, moral decisions become a matter of remaining true to our heroic nature, staying the course, often by acting to control the evil outside us. Once we discover the darkness within us, the dynamic changes. Now moral choices proceed from the knowledge that we *could* do evil, but may choose not to; the battleground is not out there but in here.

Masculine/Feminine

As men approach midlife, the gender-based aspects of heroic behavior become problematical. The masculine tendency to think of ourselves as authentic insofar as we are separate from others breaks down when we move from detached agent to finite, biological creature; the active mode of creation, directed outward so as to make separate products, is imperiled by the growing sense of embeddedness within various relational systems; rationality and the solving of objectified "problems," shedding light from our intellect out onto the dark corners of the world, become less viable when the darkness inside begins to make itself felt; the competitive drive to win, to define success by how well we control others, becomes more complicated as our awareness of kinship with other creatures in nature presses harder on us.

Reassessing the weight of what we now call gendered elements within the hero is a part of at least one kind of ancient hero story. The second self is complementary to the hero in many ways, but not least in the prominence of traits the Greeks would have thought of as characteristic of women. Enkidu, the wild man fashioned by the gods to be a companion for Gilgamesh, is in tune, as women were thought to be, with the rhythms of nature—something to be controlled by heroic males. He dresses in animal skins and has long hair "like a woman" (*The Epic of Gilgamesh* I.2.38). Patroclus presents a similar kind of contrast to Achilles' overbearing masculinity, honoring solicitude for his friends over his desire for honor, compassionate where his friend is solipsistic, defining himself through relationships rather than through the lonely, competitive absolutes of Achilles. In both of these cases, the hero's final evolution toward maturity and spiritual integration is marked by an acceptance within himself of those very "feminine" qualities embodied by his second self.

The traditional hero story could, then, accommodate a re-assessment of the masculine/feminine polarity within the hero as part of his spiritual evolution toward maturity. We have already observed that *Oedipus Rex* presents a particularly rich realization of this story type, with Tiresias as a kind of complementary second self to Oedipus: To the king's active, rational, outwardly-probing agency, he opposes a power based on his role as a passive conduit for the god's will. Oedipus looks out at the world and imposes meaning on it, while Tiresias's blindness is emblematic of a mysterious inner wisdom, often riddling and obscure. Oedipus creates by acting out into an objectified world, Tiresias carries knowledge within himself, gestating a new Oedipus, reflecting the defining power of natural forces from which the masculine hero is customarily detached. Blinding himself, Oedipus turns toward the feminine model of knowing and being that is embodied in the play by the sexually ambiguous prophet.

Engagement/Detachment

Chasing the Dream in early adulthood, we face outward; we confront the world from a position of autonomous separation. The playful, dreamy fantasies of childhood give way now before the imperative to create ourselves and our lives through exerting our will. This orientation Levinson calls "attachment"; we will call it "engagement." It does not mean that we are engaged with others in a relational sense, defining ourselves through our connections to them. On the contrary, this kind of engagement works against recognition of personal relationships as definitive; rather, we define ourselves by acting outward from a position of autonomy. At the same time, the other side of this polarity, detachment, does not necessarily entail loneliness or isolation; indeed, engagement, as we have defined it, is more likely to foster isolation, encouraging us to see ourselves as separate, self-created units. Instead, detachment means turning inward, disengaging from the outer world to look within ourselves and reenter the realm of imagination and dreams. As we approach midlife, the early adult balance (or imbalance) between the two parts of this polarity must change. All the forces pushing us then toward a recognition of our place within various larger structures foster a need to turn inward—to make the journey into darkness to confront and evaluate what is inside us.

The hero's position with regard to this polarity is, as we have seen, strongly on the side of engagement. Surging out into the world to work his will, he is often portrayed as disastrously out of touch with his inner nature. His customary mode of power is what we (following McClelland) have called stage three—understanding himself as powerful insofar as he is the source of power and the outside world is its object. And the hero is almost always a lonely man, isolated by his fierce desire for autonomy. Odysseus is the foremost example of this heroic trait: he has no real friends and feels powerful only insofar as he withholds information about himself, through disguise and lies, while manipulating others to make themselves vulnerable to him.

Oedipus, as usual, shows us the implications of this position with special acuteness, highlighting in particular its consequences for identity. Not only, until the Corinthian persona dies, does he face resolutely outward, he has no direct access to the truths he might find if he *did* look inward. Splitting the two personae of Oedipus as he does, Sophocles objectifies what is subjective in us and helps us see the outlines of our own dualities. Once again, Tiresias is the key to a new orientation toward the polarity in Oedipus. As prophet, he carries within himself what Oedipus might find if he could change the balance; blind, he embodies the inner-looking attitude that grows more prominent as the heroic perspective fades.

Oedipus at Midlife

We have been tracking a confluence of metaphors. Saying neither that fitting the template of modern psychology over *Oedipus Rex* yields some deeper truth about the work of art, nor that refracting the modern metaphors through the prism of the play reveals *their* true meaning, we have rather been using both sets of metaphors, ancient and modern, as they interact with each other and as they point beyond, to help us approach something other than either—the experience of an evolving sense of self-in-the-world as it may flow by us in life. The very act of this reading has heroic overtones, as we have seen, because the experience in itself can never be directly accessible to us as something fixed. Everything is always changing, and snapshots of experience impose form—and thus meaning—on what is never still. Though one model may seem to correspond to what we experience as "life" more closely than another, all meaning is finally metaphorical, and so ranking metaphors is problematical.

This much said, what have we learned? Sophocles has presented us with a particular lens that has allowed us to broaden and deepen the import of what the psychological phrase "midlife crisis" describes. Coming to the transition that occurs in our late thirties, we may also be playing out the implications of a powerful mode of perception, adopted in the transition from adolescence to early adulthood, driven by a mix of nature and culture. This angle of vision, as Sophocles' metaphors tell us, encompasses profound assumptions about how we become who we are, how we fit in the world—and what, finally, our lives mean—and its passing can occasion enormous changes in our ideas about our very identity and existence. *Oedipus Rex*, like many hero stories, presents the transition as a symbolic death, splitting the two "lives" of the king in a way that suggests that "Oedipus" cannot encompass both the Corinthian and the Theban at the same time: one must perish before another can live. Our modern metaphors, attuned to the interior experience of evolving identity, can accommodate some sense of enduring continuity behind the personae of the life cycle, but the subjectivity of our model diminishes the clarity of the stages of evolution. What both paradigms suggest to us is that any perspective on our identity is inextricably bound up with, on the one hand, our sense of where we fit in the world, and on the other with what we understand to be the meaning of our lives.

Conclusion: Beyond Heroism

In his last moments on the stage, Oedipus reviews his past with horror, and looks to the future of his children, entrusting them to Creon. For himself, he begs exile:

As for me,
never condemn the city of my fathers
to house my body, not while I'm alive, no,
let me live on the mountains, on Cithaeron,
my favorite haunt, I have made it famous.
Mother and father marked out that tomb—buried alive.
Mother and father marked out that rock
to be my everlasting tomb—buried alive.
Let me die there, where they tried to kill me.

(1451–1454)

There is in this plea a recognition of his place in nature, of the futility of heroic detachment from the rest of the cosmos. Finally, he would be one of the mountain-dwelling creatures that the chorus of *Antigone* saw as proper objects for human control. He, and we, have come full circle. By solving the riddle of the Sphinx—a dangerous female force—Oedipus ascended to the heroic plane of existence; acting from that detached place, he chased and captured his buried self, and in the discovery has come to understand anew the riddle's question, "What is a human being?"

At the same time, there remains in Oedipus a resistance to what his discoveries seem to have taught him: he is somehow still *different*:

Oh but this I know: no sickness can destroy me,
nothing can. I would never have been saved
from death—I have been saved
for something great and terrible, something strange.
Well let my destiny come and take me on its way!

(1455–1458)

We can never know whether Sophocles points to the "sequel" here. In twenty years, he will stage one, taking us beyond the traditional hero story into territory uncharted elsewhere in ancient literature. The result would seem to respond to Levinson's summary of what has happened in *Oedipus Rex*:

Every man in the Mid-life transition starts to see that the hero of the fairy tale does not enter a life of eternal, simple happiness. He sees, indeed, that the hero is a youth who must die or be transformed as early adulthood comes to an end. A man must begin to grieve and accept the symbolic death of the youthful hero within himself. He will gradually discover which of the qualities he can keep, which new qualities he can discover and develop in himself, and how he might be a hero of a different kind in the context of middle adulthood. (215)

When Oedipus walks back onstage, he is well beyond middle adulthood: he is old, and ready to die. Blind, led by a child, he reminds us of no one so much as of his old nemesis Tiresias. But in the figure of the old prophet, we can begin to see how Sophocles imagined a way of understanding oneself that follows directly from the limitations of the traditional heroic vision. Tiresias presents, as we have seen, a marked contrast to the kind of existence the Corinthian Oedipus embodied. At the same time, as prophet, with a special closeness to the divine, he is also different from ordinary humans: he stands nearer the boundary between human and divine, and in this he is akin to the hero. But Tiresias also shares this *liminal* position with all of us who are coming to the ends of our lives. To understand what Sophocles saw after heroism, that is where we must begin.

3

APOLLO'S GIFT

Oedipus at Colonus I

"Cosmic" consciousness is a release from self-consciousness, that is to say from the fixed belief and feeling that
one's organism is an absolute and separate thing, as dis-
tinct from a convenient unit of perception.

Alan Watts, *This Is It*

From stage left, a familiar sight: an old man, leaning on a young
woman, shuffles tentatively into view. His voice, we imagine, is
thin and raspy:

My child, child of the blind old man—Antigone,
where are we now? What land, what city of men?
Who will receive the wandering Oedipus today?
Not with gifts but a pittance . . . it's little I ask
and get still less, but quite enough for me.
Acceptance—that is the great lesson suffering teaches,
suffering and the long years, my close companions,
yes, and nobility too, my royal birthright.

(1–8)

Twenty years and more have passed since Oedipus walked out
of sight in Thebes, off the stage in Athens, and we see the evidence of their harshness, in his ragged clothes, but even more in

93

his meek demeanor. The proud tyrant, shamed but still insistent, led away from his children with difficulty, has given way to a different presence. The first three words in the Greek text set the tone for the portrait to follow: *teknon* (child) *tuphlou* (of the blind) *gerontos* (old man). Oedipus has a short way left on his life journey; his blindness has taught him a new vision that will finally lead him to his mysterious end, but first he must turn to face his past through his children.

Gouging out his eyes, Oedipus moved toward the figure of Tiresias. In that symbolic gesture, we saw the first glimmer of acceptance of what the prophet embodied—a way of being that contrasted radically with the heroic persona Oedipus had nurtured in Thebes. Now that new perspective has matured in the crucible of suffering, becoming the lesson that Oedipus has learned: acceptance of what the world gives, not heroic defiance. He cites three teachers that have led him to his new wisdom: suffering, time, and his birthright, his biological self *(to gennaion)*. To learn from these teachers would not have been possible for the former Oedipus, the Corinthian Oedipus. Traditional heroes are defined by their ability to overcome the world, not endure it; time, the measure of mortality, is to be defied; what we are given at birth is secondary to the hero we create by acting out into the world.

We might say that Oedipus sounds a familiar theme here: after all, those who learn—or ought to learn—through suffering are thick on the ground in Greek tragedy. But in this play, Sophocles goes beyond the *recognition* of suffering as teacher. Taking up where *Oedipus Rex* leaves off, the story of Oedipus's last day will show us how the old man fulfills the promise of his self-blinding by moving beyond the seeming impasse of traditional heroic self-creation and inevitable self-destruction to the new kind of empowerment that Tiresias embodies. Seeking his death, he gives new meaning to his life.

The Old Man as Stranger

Oedipus is anxious: whose city have they reached? where are they? He and Antigone are strangers to the place and must depend on the kindness of the locals. As the stranger arriving in a strange land, Oedipus replays a common story pattern in Greek literature. Like Odysseus washing up on the shores of some unknown people, he feels vulnerable, and must proceed with care. At the same time, he repeats his debut as a young man in Thebes, and here as there his advent will bring profound change to the community. But having bested the Sphinx, he was arriving in triumph, ready to take the queen and create his heroic persona. Now—old, blind, feeble—he comes already freighted with a notoriously tainted past, and may well be driven out of Athens as he was driven out of Thebes.

In his seeming weakness and dependency, Oedipus looks like the typical old man in Greek tragedy. That world, ruled by the traditional heroic perspective, finds nothing redeeming in old men. Physically diminished, they can no longer work their will in the world; withered and slowed, they show the marks of time, the hero's enemy. A reverence for older men, in deference to their wisdom and experience, is seldom evident in Greek tragic drama. Much more common is the specter presented later by the chorus of this play:

Show me the man who longs to live a day beyond his time
     who turns his back on a decent length of life,
I'll show the world a man who clings to folly.
For the long, looming days lay up a thousand things
closer to pain than pleasure, and the pleasures disappear,
     you look and know not where
when a man's outlived his limit, plunged in age
and the good comrade comes who comes at last to all,

not with a wedding-song, no lyre, no singers dancing—
the doom of the Deathgod comes like lightning
    always death at the last.

    Not to be born is best
when all is reckoned in, but once a man has seen the light
    the next best thing, by far, is to go back
back where he came from, quickly as he can.
For once his youth slips by, light on the wing
lightheaded. . . what mortal blows can he escape
    what griefs won't stalk his last days?
Envy and enemies, rage and battles, bloodshed
and last of all despised old age overtakes him,
stripped of power, companions, stripped of love—
the worst this life of pain can offer,
    old age our mate at last.

                           (1211–1238)

A notable exception to this dismal portrait is, of course, Tiresias, in whom we see a vivid example of McClelland's fourth stage of power. Whereas the hero—embodying the third stage—is the source of a power expressed on its object (the external world), the prophet is neither source nor object. He expresses power, but not his own; he embodies the god's power as it passes through him, not as it is impressed on him. Oedipus too, as we will see, can have access to this kind of power, but only after further trials.

A Sense of Place

Sophocles' last play is pervaded by a specific sense of *place*. From Oedipus's first questions to his last exit the *location* of people and things is crucial. Antigone's answer to her father's open-

ing speech describes the towers of Athens in the distance and
the immediate surroundings, which are surely sacred:

> . . . but this is holy ground
> you can sense it clearly. Why, it's bursting
> with laurel, olives, grapes, and deep in its heart,
> listen . . . nightingales, the rustle of wings—
> they're breaking into song.

$$(16–18)$$

The tender gaze of the poet may be discerned here. Sophocles was born in Colonus, and the reverence for its holiness has
a valedictory tone. Beyond this, the plants and birds all carry a
specific symbolism. Laurel is sacred to Apollo, Oedipus's patron; olives to Athena, the guardian of Athens; grapes to Dionysus, god of Greek drama. And the nightingale traditionally sings
laments for the dead. All of these elements are to return in the
chorus's first song, in praise of Colonus, but here they set the
scene economically for the last day of Apollo's most famous
ward, and of one of Athens's three great tragic poets.

Antigone eases her father to a seat on a rocky ledge just at the
edge of the grove she has described. They speculate further on
where they are: Athens they know about, but not this place;
Oedipus is especially keen to find a sacred grove; he knows they
have a mission to complete in such a place. Just as Antigone is
about to reconnoiter, a man arrives, a citizen of Colonus as it
happens. His first reaction to a friendly greeting from Oedipus
is alarm: Oedipus must move immediately; he is trespassing on
sacred ground. It is, we learn, the grove sacred to the "Terrible
Goddesses, daughters of Earth and Darkness," also known as
"the Kindly Ones, the Eumenides" (39–42). This is welcome
news to Oedipus:

Oh—

then let them receive their suppliant with kindness!
I shall never leave my place in this new land,
this is my refuge!

(44–45)

This grove, Oedipus says, is the "token" of his destiny, the
place he has been looking for. Pressing excitedly, he asks for
more details: What is this place? Who lives here? What kind of
government? The grove is sacred to the Eumenides, it seems, but
also to Poseidon and Prometheus; it has within it the Brazen
Threshold of Athens, and the surrounding settlement is called
Colonus, after a local hero whose equestrian statue is nearby;
King Theseus rules Athens and Colonus. Oedipus asks the man
to bring Theseus, to tell him, "with a small service he may gain
a great deal" (72). The man wonders what a blind man could
offer a king, to which, Oedipus: "Whatever I say, there will be a
great vision/in every word I say" (74).

Now we begin to see that Oedipus may be neither as alien nor
as impotent as he first appeared. This place has some destined role
in his life, and he in turn can offer something of value to its people. Once the citizen has left, he bursts forth in passionate prayer:

You queens of terror, faces filled with dread!
Since yours is the first holy ground
where I've sat down to rest in this new land,
I beg you, don't be harsh to Apollo, harsh to me.
When the god cried out those lifelong prophecies of doom
he spoke of *this* as well, my promised rest
after hard years weathered—
I will reach my goal, he said, my haven
where I find the grounds of the Awesome Goddesses

and make their home my home. There I will round
the last turn in the torment of my life:
a blessing to the hosts I live among,
disaster to those who sent me, drove me out!
And he warned me signs of all these things will come
in earthquake, thunder perhaps, or the flashing bolt of Zeus.

And now I know it, now some omen from you, my queens,
some bird on the wing that fills my heart with faith
has led my slow steps home to your green grove.
Yes, how else could you be the first I've met
in all the roads I've traveled?—you and I,
ascetic and sober, we who drink no wine—
or found this solemn seat, this raw unhewn rock?
Now, goddesses, just as Apollo's voice foretold,
grant my life at last some final passage,
some great consummation at the end.
Unless—who knows?—I am beneath your dignity,
slave as I am to the worst relentless pains
that ever plagued a man. Come, hear my prayer,
you sweet daughters born of primeval Darkness!
Hear me, city named for mighty Athena—Athens,
honored above all cities on the earth!
Pity this harried ghost of a man,
this Oedipus . . . Oedipus is no more
the flesh and blood of old.

(84–110)

In this speech, Oedipus's fictive life on the Athenian stage
comes together to form a single arc, from his birth, through his
heroic youth, to his death. The grove of the Eumenides is where
it will all end, and this was destined from his youth. There is

much to learn from the prayer, about the immediate present and future, about the whole shape of the life.

Oedipus will die in the grove—soon, it would appear—but not before some great "consummation," signaled by thunder and lightning from Zeus. His presence here will help his friends and harm his enemies, making him a paradigm for a traditional morality that was still prevalent in Athens and informs several of Sophocles' plays. That the grove should be sacred to these goddesses in particular is telling. They are earth deities, as opposed to the Olympian gods, and characteristically associated with death. But further, as daughters of earth and darkness, they represent those forces that the Corinthian Oedipus tried to deny in his life. Sending him to these divine guardians for his last great act, Apollo would seem to confirm the change in perspective signaled by the self-blinding: to become the man he is to be, to complete his journey, Oedipus must face the darkness. And finally, we note that the Eumenides, also called the Furies, are the deities assigned specifically to guarding blood ties, and hounding those who dishonor them. That Oedipus is destined to die in the grounds sacred to these spirits suggests some measure of reconciliation and healing at the close of his painful life.

Crossing Boundaries

Oedipus ends his prayer as a chorus of elders from Colonus appear. Hiding in the grove, he hears their first words, which are not promising:

Look for the man! Who is he? where's he hiding?—
where's he gone, rushed away, where now?
    That man, of all men on earth
the most shameless, desperate man alive!
Look for him, press the search now

scour every inch of the ground!
    A wanderer, wandering fugitive
that old man—no native, a stranger
else he'd never set foot where none may walk,
this grove of the Furies, irresistible, overwhelming—
Oh we tremble to say their names, filing by,
not a look, not a sound, not a word
moving our lips in silence
silent reverence, oh pass by, pass by. . .
    but now one's come, the rumors say
who fears the Furies not at all—
the man we look for, scanning,
round and round this holy precinct,
cannot find him
               cannot find his hiding . . .

                         (117–137)

    The old men's suspicious, anxious tone reminds us how pre-
carious Oedipus's foothold still is in this fateful place. To these
ordinary citizens, the old man represents something alien and so
to be feared: he is still "the stranger," and may be driven out.
Emerging from the grove, Oedipus does little to calm the ex-
cited crowd. They find him "dreadful" to look at; he begs them
not to see him as *anomos* (an outlaw)—the threat of exclusion
abides; who *is* he? Not exactly a fortunate man, he says, given
that he is blind. The fact of his blindness excites still more anxious curiosity: was he blind at birth? He has obviously suffered,
and they want to help him avoid more pain:

        You've gone too far, too far—
but before you stumble one step more
invading the sacred glade, rapt in silence

the deep green lawns where the bowl brims libations
running with holy water swirling honey—
                    Stop—
sufferer, stranger, you must not trespass!
Move, come down among us now—
closer, a good safe way from the grove,
            you hear, old traveler, man of grief?
Do you have an appeal to make before our session?
Move!—move off forbidden ground, come down
where the law permits us all to speak,
till then hold back
      be silent, not a word!

                                        (155–169)

   Oedipus is reluctant to leave the grove, but the chorus reassures him: they will never drag him away from his resting place,
if only he will leave the sacred precinct. There follows a passage
of some twenty-five lines in which Oedipus gropes his way to a
place that satisfies the old men, who sound like a bomb squad
disarming a dangerous device: Oedipus becomes in this passage
a charged *object*, his physicality almost numinous. Proximity to
the sacred grove appears to energize the old exile, as if the power
of the goddesses runs through him there, and when he moves
away from the sacred place, leaning on Antigone, he seems to
shrink, to revert from the passionate pilgrim of the prayer to the
weary, feeble old man we saw enter at the play's beginning. Modern psychological paradigms offer a perspective that deepens the
impact of these first scenes.

                    Modern Metaphors
   As we have seen, studies of the psychology of aging make a
distinction between the position of old men in industrial, and

postindustrial, cultures and their status in more traditional cultures. The former situation tends to produce a strongly negative portrait of old men; in the latter, the image is more positive. This should not be surprising, given the glorification in Western culture of the heroic conquest of nature—of the enthronement there of competitive virtues that lead to success as defined in the old, masculine heroic model. David Gutmann, a pioneer in the cross-cultural study of aging, puts the distinction in a wider context that touches on many issues the first scene of the play has raised (Gutmann 1977, 315–316):

[S]ocieties that sponsor an egocentric, self-seeking spirit in the population will be lethal to young and old alike. But societies which sponsor altruism, and the formation of internalized objects, provide security to these venerable cohorts. The internal object, an emotionally invested re-presentation abstracted from a long history of shared interaction, has constancy and relates the past to the present. Accordingly, the older person who has acquired true object status transcends his immediate condition. His child does not see in the parent a useless, ugly person. Rather, he still relates to the vigorous, sustaining parent he once knew, as well as the weak person immediately before him. By keeping his object status the older person avoids becoming the *stranger*, and is thereby protected against the fear and revulsion aroused by the "other." There is a much noted tendency for the aged to reminisce, and even to relive their earlier life. Though taken as a sign of eccentricity, this may be an adaptive move to escape the lethal condition of "otherness." As they reminisce, the elders seem to be saying, "See me not as I am, but as a total *history*, and as someone who was once like you."

Faced with dismissal by a culture that honors heroic values above all others, the old man depends for his authority on the perception that he somehow retains his youthful self in the continuities of his personal history. A less precarious prospect may await old men in more traditional cultures not dominated by the self-seeking, competitive spirit. There, passive affiliation with the supernatural tends to replace in old men the dependence on physical strength as a source of leverage. This change, combined with the obvious fact that the old are closer to the mysteries of death and thus the world of spirits, can make the old man a kind of intermediary between humans and gods:

Precisely *because* of their frailty, the aged are moving into the country of the dead; they take on some of the fearsome aura of the corpse they will soon become. Furthermore, in old age, a strong spirit is revealed in its own terms, no longer masked by the vitality of a young body. Thus, besides intersecting the mythic past, the aged overlap the spirit world which they will soon enter; and as they blend with that world they acquire its essential physiognomy and powers. . . . Clearly, the old traditionalist's power does not depend on his ability to dominate men, but on his ability to influence God. (314)

This picture of empowerment for old men follows directly from the change in perspective we saw at the end of *Oedipus Rex*. Moving from active agency to passive affiliation with transcendent powers is consistent with moving from seeing the meaning of one's life as the product of the imposing of one's will on the external world to a recognition of one's place within larger structures of meaning. In old age, the issues are more sharply focused, because old men are usually thought of as closer to the transcendent forces than middle-aged men, but the relationship between identity, power, and life's meaning in the old man is only the final maturing of a perspective that follows from the death

of the Dream. By telling the story of old Oedipus's last day,
Sophocles can bring these relationships to a characteristically
vivid expression that completes his dramatic picture of the
meaning of a masculine life.

Oedipus's situation does not offer a clear path to the power
of the old hero. Though Gutmann casts the dilemma of the
stranger in a family drama, it is easy enough to see how it reaches
beyond that milieu. Oedipus is in the role of stranger within
what looks like the normal heroic world of Greek tragedy,
friendly to self-seeking and egocentricity. And in his case, "object status" is hardly available to counterbalance the fear of otherness: continuity with his past self is not a plus for Oedipus. Indeed, Oedipus's major challenge in seeking a good death will be
to finish up his business with the past, and *Oedipus at Colonus* is
in some respects a reprise of *Oedipus Rex.*

At the same time, the opening scenes of the drama show in
Oedipus the potential for passive mastery. His destined affiliation with the Eumenides seems to empower him: the closer he is
to their sacred precinct, the more energized he becomes. He begins to exemplify in this sense McClelland's fourth stage of
power, acting as a vehicle for divine forces that are beyond his
control or understanding. The object of these powers is to be
Athens, the city to which Oedipus can offer some as-yet unde-
fined gift, the friends he will help at the expense of his enemies.
The key to his achieving a final "consummation" will be in realizing the potential—first glimpsed in the complementary figure of Tiresias—that his bond to the Eumenides offers; the ob-
stacles are those parts of his life that threaten to drag him back
into the lethal milieux of Thebes and his family, where the
heroic mode of being would make him a powerless pawn in the
futile struggles of others. Tracking his progress allows us to
learn from it a way of flourishing beyond youthful heroism—

perhaps of achieving some consummation of our own in the completion of life.

Back From the Edge

Oedipus sits on the edge of the sacred precinct, and we feel the *liminality* of the old man. The boundary of the grove, so concretely present in nervous stage business, also symbolizes other levels of meaning: Oedipus is about to die, and the grove stands for the country of the dead; paradoxically its sacred quality also makes the green glade a metaphor for the mysterious existence of the gods, bounded off from the human world of death and change. Like the youthful hero who presses against the boundaries of divinity, Oedipus, by his position on the edge of the grove, helps to define the complex meaning of human experience by showing its contours. The difference is that Oedipus does not confuse himself with the gods. He is powerful because his proximity makes him an apt vessel for transcendent powers, not their replacement. In the physical movements of these first scenes, Sophocles presents us with a spiritual geography of the drama. Final greatness for Oedipus lies within the sacred grove, with all that it symbolizes; from now until that final moment, forces friendly and hostile will pull Oedipus toward and away from the boundary, physical and metaphysical, of the grove: he will not leave the stage until the very end of the play. The contest begins with innocent curiosity in the chorus.

The old man has been safely moved, and the chorus can treat him as they would any other stranger, asking for information: who were his parents; what is his fatherland? Oedipus responds to these seemingly innocuous questions with evasion. Pressed further, he becomes abject: "No no! Don't ask who I am—/no more probing, testing—stop—no more!" (210–211). The old men are undeterred, and after a lengthy hesitation Oedipus reveals his identity. His worst fears are realized in the reaction:

LEADER:

You, you're *that* man——?

OEDIPUS:

Please, don't be afraid, whatever I say—

LEADER:

O—ohhh!

OEDIPUS:

My destiny, very hard. . . .

Antigone, what will they do to us now?

LEADER:

Out with you! Out of our country—far away!

(222–226)

In this moment Oedipus reverts from numinous pilgrim to threatening alien. His identity, instead of reassuring the citizens, heightens his aura of otherness in their eyes: he is a famous outcast, polluted by his parricide and incest, someone who cannot even be *touched*. Oedipus's past offers no solace to him or others; its appearance here begins a long interlude in the play's structure, as Oedipus is pulled away from the edge of his mortal life and back into the troubles of this world.

We have witnessed a replay of the recognition scene from *Oedipus Rex*. In both plays the revealing of Oedipus's "true" identity brings horror to the citizens of his chosen city; in both, the result is threatened exile. That the scene comes so early in this play signals an unconventional structure: the usual position is just before the dramatic climax of the story. But if we look at the entire story behind the first play, a certain similarity appears between the two works. In each, Oedipus arrives at a strange city, apparently an alien; subsequent events reveal that he has, in fact, an important connection with the new place—a bond that is finally more enduring than his ties to his "home"; in each, the issue of Oedipus's identity is central to a dramatic meditation on the meaning of life.

In the aftermath of the dramatic revelation, Antigone pleads for compassion: her father, as they can see, is *athlion* (shattered); she and he throw themselves on the citizens' mercy, appealing to them as if to a god. *Oedipus at Colonus* fits into a subgenre of Greek tragedy called "suppliant drama"—plays about exiles arriving in another community and depending for their salvation on the kindness of strangers. In this case, the motif proceeds on two levels. Antigone and Oedipus need the protection of Athens, as it turns out, but finally the old man's haven will be provided by the Kindly Ones in their sacred grove.

The chorus are moved, but they insist the strangers leave, fearing the gods. Their intransigence angers Oedipus:

Then what's the good of glory, magnificent renown,
if in its flow it streams away to nothing?
If Athens, Athens
is that rock of reverence all men say it is,
the only city on earth to save the ruined stranger,
the only one to protect him, give him shelter—
where are such kindnesses for me? First
you raise me up from my seat in the grove,
then you drive me off the land, terrified
by my name alone, surely not my physique
nor what I've done.
                    Since *my* acts, at least,
were acts of suffering more than actions outright—
but I cannot bear to tell you the whole story
of mother and father . . .
that's what makes you fear me, well I know.
                    But no, no—
how could you call me guilty, how by nature?
I was attacked, I struck in self-defense.

Why even if I had known what I was doing,
how could that make me guilty? But in fact,
knowing nothing, no, I went . . . the way I went—
but the ones who made me suffer, they knew full well,
they wanted to destroy me.

(258–274)

Here Sophocles begins a review of the moral issues raised in *Oedipus Rex*, that will continue throughout the central section of the play. The years have not dulled Oedipus's memories, nor his feelings about what happened, but the first waves of self-loathing have been replaced by a greater sense of his victimization: how could he be guilty, if he acted in ignorance? He reacted to a challenge on the road, and took what Thebes offered him, but all unknowing. Oedipus's defense follows conventional lines, and we can see in it the traces of the legal thinking that developed in the fifth century in Athens, as an older standard of justice, which devalued intent and concentrated on acts, gave way to a more complex perspective. Although the word "guilty" in the translation fits our modern notions of legal accountability, it may blur slightly what is at stake here. The Greek phrase is *kakos phusin*, which might be rendered "evil by nature," and in using it Oedipus raises questions about the relationship between character and action. Is he a bad person if he acted in ignorance, no matter what the result?

The question of Oedipus's guilt or innocence is no easier to answer here than it is in *Oedipus Rex*, and, finally, no more relevant to our particular purposes. The *context* within which this review occurs *is* important to us. What is the meaning of Oedipus's behavior in the light of our interest in the evolving picture of his understanding of himself and his relationship to the world?

We notice, first of all, that thinking about the past, though initially daunting, eventually angers Oedipus, and that anger invigorates him: the feeble, querulous old man the chorus edged out of the grove has been replaced by someone more assertive. Modern studies of aging suggest that pugnacity in old men keeps them alive. In particular, the ability to externalize conflicts: "Integral to active mastery, and perhaps to longevity, is the capacity to externalize aggression, to turn potentially debilitating inner conflicts into external struggles. This author has observed that surviving traditionalists frequently complain about a faceless 'someone' who is trying to rob or kill them. In some cases the enemy is clearly a metaphor of death" (Gutmann 308–309). Seen in this context, Oedipus's anger is illuminating. His final goal is to make a good death in the grove of the Eumenides; to do so will be to realize the fruits of his mature self, the new understanding of the meaning of his life within the larger structures of the cosmos. In the metaphors of modern psychology, he will exhibit passive mastery in achieving his final consummation. Yet faced with the facts of his past, he becomes more *active*, in a certain sense. His anger seems to pull his attention toward forces outside himself that he believes have victimized him. The spiritual map is enriched: moving away from the sacred grove takes Oedipus out of the present moment and into the past—and, as we will see, into the tangled web of his family history that, instead of ensuring his continued safety through the preservation of "object status," renders him vulnerable. As is often the case, this feeling of weakness is covered over by a less frightening emotion, anger, that energizes the old man and puts death off.

We see a set of polarities emerging. On one side, the present moment, colored by the prospect of a glorious finale in a sacred place that symbolizes timeless transcendence. That end will realize the promise of Oedipus's passive mastery, his role as selfless vehicle for powers greater than he. On the other side, the past, informed by competitive, heroic willfulness. Plunging back into that past and away from his destined end first stirs fear in Oedipus, which is followed by an active aggression, a desire to project his darker self out onto those transcendent forces, defining against them his separate ego. Reviewing his past seems to cut Oedipus off from his newfound numinous power, and he reverts to the tactics that worked for the heroic king of Thebes.

Finally it all comes back to power and its relationship to personal authenticity. The Corinthian Oedipus felt powerful and authentic insofar as he imposed his will on the world; the aged Oedipus has no need of this agency, because the gods have guaranteed his empowerment, if he will fulfill *their* will. The conflict in *Oedipus Rex* between the Corinthian Oedipus and the Theban Oedipus appears to resurface in this play, adding a further dimension to the story. What appears to be a struggle for the *body* of the old man becomes, on another level, a contest to define once and for all the meaning of his life.

Family History

Oedipus, ending his self-defense with a plea for sanctuary, repeats his assertion that he can offer something in return:

Don't reject me as you look into the horror
of my face, these sockets raked and blind.
I come as someone sacred, someone filled
with piety and power, bearing a great gift
for all your people. And when your ruler comes,
whoever is your leader, you will hear it all
and know it all, and meanwhile
as we wait together, do not be unjust.

(285–291)

We might recognize a plea for something akin to "object status" here: see me not as I appear, but as something *more*; do not
put me in the deadly category of "other," but see me as someone
who is connected to you. The chorus, characteristically cautious, will not make a commitment until Theseus comes. At this
moment, a figure appears in the distance—a woman in a broad-
brimmed hat. Antigone recognizes her sister, Ismene, who has
arrived from Thebes. After an emotional reunion, Ismene reveals that she brings bad news. How are the boys, asks Oedipus,
seeming to sense that the trouble lies with them. Ismene is eva-
sive: "They are—/where they are . . . now's their darkest hour."
(336). This brings from Oedipus a lengthy denunciation of
both sons—lazy and inattentive to their father, in contrast to
his daughters, loyal and strong, Antigone traveling with him, Ismene serving as his agent in Thebes. We see again the unhappy
condition of Oedipus, a father who is unable to count on love
and support from his own sons, an old man whose reminiscing
brings only pain.

Pressed for more details, Ismene tells what the trouble is, and
why it will affect Oedipus. The younger son, Eteocles, has driven
the older, Polynices, off the throne and out of Thebes; Polynices has taken refuge in Argos, where marriage to the king's
daughter ensures him allies in the battle to come for the throne
in Thebes. New oracles suggest that Thebes "will want you
greatly,/once you are dead, and even while you're alive—/they
need you for their survival." (388–390); "They are in your
hands, the oracles says,/their power rests in you." (392). It
seems that his tomb will curse the Thebans, if it lacks the proper
rites. They want him back, but not within the city limits—since
he is ritually unclean—but only nearby, where they can control
him; Creon is coming even now to take him back to Thebes.

Oedipus is enraged to hear this news and vows never to go back. In the speech that follows, we learn more about the past. At first, shamed by his incest and parricide, Oedipus wanted only to die in Thebes. After some time passed, his feelings softened and he began to see his acts in a more forgiving light. Just then, the city decided to exile him, and his sons, who could have stopped it, did nothing. The girls have saved him; the boys will never be forgiven for their treachery. Now Oedipus sees these prophecies as of a piece with the old ones: if Athens and the Eumenides will defend him, the city will be rewarded; Thebes, meanwhile, will be punished for driving him out. The full story of the prophecies is teased out over the course of the play, but this much is clear: Oedipus, once helpless in the hands of the Thebans, now has the city in his power; his leverage over them depends on the physical location of his body while he lives and after he dies.

The pattern that began with Oedipus's first self-defense continues. Reminded of his past by news of his family, Oedipus feels ashamed, but as he reviews the events and his part in them, anger crowds out shame, and he becomes more assertive, seeing his troubles as the result of others—his disloyal sons; the treacherous citizens of Thebes. An interlude now punctuates yet another replaying of this rhythm: the chorus require Oedipus to perform certain rites in the grove, to ensure the goodwill of the goddesses; he asks Ismene to take his place, as he is too weak and feeble to do what is needed. We are back to the passive, frail old man of the play's opening scene, who reemerges when called away from the sources of anger. When Ismene leaves, the chorus begin to ask more questions. They've heard rumors about Oedipus's past, but are they true? This brings anguish: he begs them not to put him through the agony of describing it all again; they persist, and a familiar theme emerges:

OEDIPUS:

I have suffered, friends,
the worst horrors on earth, suffered against my will,
I swear to god, not a single thing self-willed—

CHORUS:

What?—how?

OEDIPUS:

Thebes married me to disaster! Thebes bound me fast,
so blind, to a bride who was my curse, my ruin, my—

(521–526)

Further details—the incest, its issue—put Oedipus on the rack
again: "Horrible, countless horrors/sweeping over me . . . "
(536–537). But to the chorus's description of what he has *done*,
Oedipus replies firmly. He has not *done* anything, but:

Received,
received as a gift, a prize to break the heart—
Oh would to god I'd never served my city,
never won the prize they handed up to me!

(539–541)

Each time he goes back in time, the active, testy old man
eventually returns, seeing his troubles as things put upon him—
a painful gift. When the chorus push ahead to the murder of
Laius, the pattern recycles once more in miniature, from abject
pain—"the second stab" (544)—to projection:

I'll tell you:
the man I murdered—he'd have murdered me!
I am innocent! Pure in the eyes of the law,
blind, unknowing, I, I came to this!

(546–548)

Theseus

Oedipus is spared further review by the arrival of Theseus. The Athenian king knows all about the past, but why has Oedipus come to Colonus now? He reassures the old man that he will be a sympathetic audience; he, too, grew up in exile, and will never turn away a stranger. Though Sophocles does not allude to it, there is, in fact, an even greater parallel between the two men, at least in one story preserved elsewhere: Theseus, setting out for Crete to kill the Minotaur and save Athens from a yearly sacrifice of young men to that monster, promises that when he returns he will signal by the color of his sail whether he is alive (white) or dead (black). He defeats the Minotaur, but forgets to change his sail from black to white, and Aegeus commits suicide, thinking his son to be dead. Theseus, like Oedipus, grows up in exile, saves his city by conquering a monster, and inadvertently kills his own father.

The similarities between Theseus and Oedipus—though we cannot know how much the audience is supposed to add to Theseus's story—are tantalizing. They have an immediate function within the plot, reassuring the nervous old man; but beyond this, Sophocles seems to present in Theseus an alternative to the self-destructive hero of *Oedipus Rex*. Active, self-confident, powerful, he has many of the qualities of the young Oedipus, but not his insistence on controlling the world: Finishing his welcoming speech to Oedipus, he calls himself "only a man"—one who knows he has no power over what will happen tomorrow (567–568). Oedipus, swept away by gratitude, calls Theseus *gennaion* (noble), the word he used in his opening speech to describe the quality in himself that taught him acceptance instead of willful self-assertion. In reply, Theseus asks him to "teach," that he may learn (569–575). The Corinthian Oedipus could not be taught so easily.

The portrait of Theseus, promising as it is, will not be developed much further in the play, though his role as representative of Athenian virtues becomes prominent later in the story. For now, Oedipus wants only to win the king's protection. To secure it, he offers himself:

I come with a gift for you,
my own shattered body . . . no feast for the eyes,
but the gains it holds are greater than great beauty.

(576–578)

Now the promises of earlier scenes become more concrete. Oedipus not only brings a gift, he *is* the gift. In the ensuing exchange, he supplies details to the initially doubtful king. Thebes will one day be defeated in the place where they now stand; to avert this, Oedipus's sons want to take him away to Thebes, because the city where his grave is will win the war.

Theseus cannot imagine war between the two cities, to which Oedipus replies with a long speech affirming the power of time, which crushes and obliterates all in its path—the earth's strength, a man's body; hate turns to love and back to hate again; tranquil summer will give way to wintry war until

some far-off day when my dead body, slumbering, buried
cold in death, will drain their hot blood down,
if Zeus is still Zeus and Apollo the son of god
speaks clear and true.

(621–623)

Oedipus's final consummation is folded into the hard-won perspective that brought him to it. He will be powerful in the fullness of time, the god's servant, not one who defies time and destiny. The meaning of his life will be realized in his death.

Gifts: The Hero and the Community
Theseus is moved by the old man's offer:

Such kindness—who could reject such a man?
First, in any case, Oedipus is our ally:
by mutual rights we owe him hospitality.
What's more, he has come to beg our gods for help
and render no small benefit to our country
in return, to me as well.
So I respect his claims, I'll never reject
the gifts he offers, no, I will settle him
in our land, a fellow citizen with full rights.

And if it pleases our friend to remain here,
I command you, old men, guard him well.
But if he'd rather come along with me—
what is your pleasure, Oedipus?
The choice is yours. Whatever you decide,
I will stand behind you all the way.

(631–642)

Theseus's tone is consistent with what we have seen of him so
far. His offer is made in the context of an exchange, but the appeal to a sense of mercy and the demands of hospitality signal
an expansive generosity that goes beyond mere reciprocity. A
dispute about the Greek text of the play clouds the issue of what
exactly Oedipus's status will be in a legal sense, but the general
import of Theseus's intent is clear: he will protect the old man,
and make him part of the community in Athens. In exchange,
Athens can look forward to some future gift, the exact timing
of which still remains mysterious, from the old man. Looking
more closely at the dynamic of giving and receiving in the play

will enrich our understanding of the bond between Oedipus and his adopted city.

Lewis Hyde, in his book *The Gift*, explores the implications of giving as an *erotic* act—one that binds, in contrast to the exchanges of a market economy: "It is this element of relationship that leads me to speak of gift exchange as an 'erotic' commerce, opposing *eros* (the principle of attraction, union, involvement that binds together) to *logos* (reason and logic in general, the principle of differentiation in particular). A market economy is an emanation of *logos*" (xiv). Hyde pursues this distinction in myriad ways. At the heart of the gift economy are movement, bonding, and paradox: to remain a gift, an object must always move, and as it moves it brings with it increase—an increase opposed to the "increase" realized from a sale in a market economy, which stays behind as profit. The increase begins when the gift has moved *through* someone, when a gift circle appears; at the same time, the gift must always be consumed in order to maintain its abundance: it is property that "perishes" for the person giving, and in this death it brings new life for both the giver and the receiver. The spirit of the gift increases because the body of the gift is consumed; the mere passage of the gift, the act of donation, contains the feeling, and therefore the passage alone is the investment.

Of particular interest to us are the implications of gift exchange as a foundation for community. Many tribal societies, it seems, use the circulation of gifts as the cement that binds people together. In this venue, giving becomes more than reciprocity between two parties:

Reciprocal giving is a form of gift exchange, but it is the simplest. The gift moves in a circle, and two people do not make much of a circle. This is why . . . most of the stories of exchange have a minimum of three people. . . . Circular giving differs from reciprocal giving in several ways. First, when the gift moves in a circle no one ever receives it from the same person he gives it to. . . . The whole mood is different. . . . When I give to someone from whom I do not receive (and yet I do receive elsewhere), it is as if the gift goes around a corner before it comes back. I have to give blindly. And I will feel a sort of blind gratitude as well. The smaller the circle is—and particularly if it involves just two people—the more a man can keep his eyes on things and the more likely it is that he will start to think like a salesman. But so long as the gift passes out of sight it cannot be manipulated by one man or one pair of gift partners. When the gift moves in a circle its motion is beyond the control of the personal ego, and so the bearer must be a part of the group and each donation is an act of faith (16).

Viewed in the context of Hyde's metaphors, our play takes on new meaning. Oedipus, it seems, has something to give to the Athenians, and they can reciprocate. Yet the gift did not originate with Oedipus but with the gods—specifically Apollo, who can guarantee as no mortal can the efficacy of the gift. Already, then, we have a gift circle. Theseus, in his response to Oedipus, can be understood to offer a gift on behalf of his subjects, but the gods, not Oedipus—who will be dead—will return the gift. The Athenians give blindly, as an act of faith, and they will feel a blind gratitude. Out of this circulation of gifts will come a powerful bond between Oedipus, Athens, and the gods—a new community.

We observe that this relationship between the hero and his new community differs from the earlier, precarious alliance in Thebes. There, the city chose to participate in the formation of Oedipus's heroic dream. By doing so, Thebes staked its health on the configuration of the world that follows from the heroic vision. Oedipus became the citizens' agent in the world and their link to the gods; in return, they received the fruits of his self-assertion. But finally the bargain was a costly one. When Oedipus's heroic persona collapsed under the weight of his true identity, the civic order went down with it. Now Athens, like Thebes, will receive gifts from Oedipus, but the context is different. Instead of being an extension of the hero's egocentric perspective, the city will take part in a larger order—a gift circle that brings them into contact with the gods in a new way.

Returning to Hyde's metaphors, we see how giving and receiving can also reflect the evolution in Oedipus's understanding of his place in and relationship to the larger order of the cosmos:

I find it useful to think of the ego complex as a thing that keeps expanding, and not something to be overcome or done away with. An ego has formed and hardened by the time most of us reach adolescence, but it is small, an ego of one. Then, if we fall in love, for example, the constellation of identity expands and the ego-of-one becomes an ego-of-two. The young lover, often to his own amazement, finds himself saying "we" instead of "me." Each of us identifies with a wider and wider community as we mature, coming eventually to think and act with a group-ego (or, in most of these gift stories, a tribal ego), which speaks with the "we" of kings and wise old people. Of course the larger it becomes, the less it feels like what we usually mean by ego. Not entirely, though: whether an adolescent is thinking of himself or a nation of itself, it still feels like egotism to anyone who is not included. There is still a boundary. (16–17)

The gift can circulate at every level of the ego. In the ego-of-one we speak of self-gratification, and whether it's forced or chosen, a virtue or a vice, the mark of self-gratification is its isolation. Reciprocal giving, the ego-of-two, is a little more social. . . . But again, if the exchange goes on and on to the exclusion of others, it soon goes stale. . . . No one else can drink from the ego-of-two. It has its moment in our maturation, but it is an infant form of the gift circle. (18)

Finally, when the circle expands, the boundaries of our very ego can expand with it:

If the ego widens still further, however, it really does change its nature and become something we would no longer call ego. There is a consciousness in which we act as part of things larger even than the race. . . . There is no boundary to be outside of, unless the universe itself is bounded. (17) . . . a circulation of gifts nourishes those parts of our spirit that are not entirely personal, parts that derive from nature, the group, the race, or the gods. Furthermore, although these wider spirits are a part of us, they are not "ours"; they are endowments bestowed upon us. (38)

What Hyde is talking about here is the expansion of our idea of who we are beyond the heroic *ego* to the larger *self*. Now who we are includes "gifts" given to us by powers beyond our control, and when we pass on a gift, part of us goes with it. The most powerful realization of the gift circle is that which includes the gods (Hyde has been discussing the story of Abraham and Isaac):

The inclusion of the Lord in the circle . . . changes the ego in which the gift moves in a way unlike any other addition. It is enlarged beyond the tribal ego and beyond nature. Now . . . we would no longer call it an ego at all. The gift moves beyond all boundary and circles into mystery. . . . The passage into mystery always refreshes. . . . We are lightened when our gifts rise from pools we cannot fathom. Then we know they are not a solitary egotism and they are inexhaustible. (20)

Oedipus, old and battered, has come to see his entire life in the terms Hyde suggests. As he says in defending himself to the curious chorus, he has *suffered* his fate, not created it (266–267); Jocasta was a *gift* from the Thebans; beyond this, everything that has happened to him was given by the gods (539–541). Taking this perspective puts Oedipus squarely in line with Achilles' profound vision of humility at the end of the *Iliad*:

Such is the way the gods spun life for unfortunate mortals,
that we live in unhappiness, but the gods themselves have no sor-
    rows.
There are two urns that stand on the door-sill of Zeus. They are
    unlike
for the gifts they bestow: an urn of evils, an urn of blessings.
If Zeus who delights in thunder mingles these and bestows them
on man, he shifts, and moves now in evil, again in good fortune.
But when Zeus bestows from the urn of sorrows, he makes a failure of man, and the evil hunger drives him over the shining
earth, and he wanders respected neither of gods nor mortals.
                                        Iliad 24. 525–533

Moving beyond the heroic impasse, Oedipus has the poten-
tial to become, like Tiresias, a channel for powers greater than himself. Gifts circulate through him, bringing increase with them. As the gifts move, his very self may expand, reconfiguring the boundaries of his identity far beyond the ego-of-one that drove his heroic will in *Oedipus Rex*, moving toward what Jung would call individuation or self-completion. Seen in this light, the arguments over whether Oedipus becomes a legal citizen of

Athens are beside the point: his connection with the city and its people transcends the laws of humans. And finally, because the gods form part of the gift circle, what Oedipus brings to Athens and what he receives will circle into mystery.

But we will see that this consummation can occur only when Oedipus has finished with his past life, and the perspective that it implies. To see himself as acted upon by larger forces *can* enable Oedipus to understand himself in a new way; it can also be a part of the old, isolated, heroic self, acting out into the world to defend itself against evils "out there." One man's gift is another man's persecution; the meaning of life, as we have said, depends on where we are looking from.

Conclusion: The Community and Its Enemies

Having reassured the old man that he will be safe in his new community, Theseus hurries off to attend to affairs of state. There follows one of the most celebrated choral songs in Greek tragedy—an ode to Colonus. The ivy, laurel, olives, and narcissus that Antigone first described are returned to our attention, all signaling the special relationship of this place and its mother city Athens with the gods, Athena, Apollo, Dionysus, Aphrodite, the Eumenides, Demeter and Persephone, Poseidon, and Zeus. In Greek, the poetry is exquisite—a lyrical and tender farewell by the aged poet to his birthplace. The focus on these particular physical details takes us back to the opening scene and frames the first major movement of the play's structure. Oedipus, having arrived as a feeble, frightened stranger, has been taken into a new community, one informed by the gift circle that the old man has established with the citizens and the gods. The dynamic of this community reflects and reinforces the hard-won wisdom that began with the self-blinding and has matured in the crucible of suffering. Here, in this place, Oedipus will end his long life.

But not quite yet. There are, as we have seen, threats to this new union and to the understanding of himself that Oedipus carries into it. Echoes from the past, of Oedipus's heroic persona and its consequences, have come to be associated in this play with Thebes and with Oedipus's sons. These forces have already begun to intrude, in the reports from Ismene and the curiosity of the chorus. In the second half of the play, Oedipus will have to meet and master his past once more, turning to face it with a combative truculence that fits with that time and his former persona within it. Struggling against Creon and Polynices, Oedipus will encounter embodiments of his old self; leaving them finally behind, he will come fully into the inheritance of Tiresias, and then move beyond it.

4

BEYOND TIRESIAS

Oedipus at Colonus 2

Man, thinking of himself secretly as a completely free autonomous self, with unlimited possibilities (after all he is
taught by his society that this is what he is), finds himself
in an impossible predicament. He is "as a god" and therefore everything is within reach. But it turns out that all he
can successfully reach by his own volition is not quite
worth having. What he *really* seeks and needs—love, an authentic identity, a life that has meaning—cannot be had
merely by *willing* and by taking steps to procure them. . . .
The things we really need come to us only as gifts, and in
order to receive them as gifts we have to be open. In order
to be open we have to renounce ourselves, in a sense we
have to *die* to our image of ourselves, our autonomy, our fix-
ation upon our self-willed identity. We have to relax that
psychic and spiritual cramp that knots us in the painful,
vulnerable, helpless "I" that is all we know as ourselves.

Thomas Merton, *Conjectures of A Guilty Bystander*

Oedipus has come to Athens seeking rest, bearing gifts from the
gods. In his meeting with Theseus, he forms a bond rich with
implications for himself and for his new city. Moving beyond
reciprocity, the old man draws Athens into a gift circle with the
gods; in doing so, he begins to realize the promise of his self-

125

blinding by becoming the channel through which divine power flows, and in this he redefines the meaning of his life. Much is at stake, then, when Creon arrives from Thebes to challenge this new bond.

Creon and the Tragic Past

Creon comes freighted with meaning beyond the immediate time and place. His own history as a character in the trilogy of Oedipus plays by Sophocles is, as we have seen, a mixed one. The earliest Creon, of *Antigone*, presents the model of a tyrant in our modern sense: power-hungry, suspicious, self-destructive; in *Oedipus Rex*, a milder figure emerges—one capable of strong emotion when challenged, but also of moderation and restraint in dealing with the ruined and frightening king. Here, he walks on stage preceded, as we recall, by dark prophecies:

ISMENE:

   Yes!
 the gods are about to raise you to your feet—
 till now they were bent on your destruction.

OEDIPUS:

 It costs them little to raise an old man!
 Someone crushed in younger days.

ISMENE:

 That may be,
 but Creon, at any rate—make no mistake,
 he's coming for you, for just this reason.
 Soon, not late, I warn you.

OEDIPUS:

 To do what, my child? Be clearer—tell me.

ISMENE:

 To settle you near the fatherland of Thebes,

to have you in their power,
but you may not set foot within the borders.
OEDIPUS:
What earthly use am I to them, deposited
beyond the gates?
ISMENE:
Your tomb will curse them
if it lacks the proper rites.

(394–403)

Thebes plans to leave Oedipus in limbo, outside the city but
close by. The prophecy is obscure, like all messages from the
gods, but this much is clear: Thebes will suffer a defeat "that day
they stand upon your [Oedipus's] tomb" (411). The Thebans
seem to hope that by having Oedipus near their city, they can
somehow avoid defeat at the hands of foreigners. Oedipus, looking to find rest in the grove of the goddesses, has tied himself to
Athens, and so pledged to bring victory to that city sometime in
the future.

Creon is, then, the agent for a maneuver that looks familiar to
students of Greek tragedy and of *Oedipus Rex* in particular:
Prophecies have foretold an outcome that he and his city hope
somehow to avoid. Within the world of the play, his ploys seem
at least plausible, but to us, looking on from our detached perspective, they are of a piece with other desperate attempts to
deny the workings of inexorable forces beyond the control of
mortals. In Creon, Oedipus confronts aspects of his former
heroic self—the tragic denial of *what must be*. That Creon, too, is
an *old* man (probably older than Oedipus) reminds us that the
new perspective Oedipus is trying to bring to fruition is not necessarily the "normal" model for old men in Greek literature.
Wisdom can come through suffering, but not to everyone.

Creon begins mildly enough:

Noble old men, the pride of your land,
I seem to catch a glint of fear in your eyes,
a sudden shudder at my arrival. Don't be afraid,
and don't greet me with anything uncivil.
I haven't come here with any thought of force,
I'm too old for that,
and I know the city I have reached is strong,
if any city in Greece is strong—a great power.
No, I have been sent, despite my age,
to persuade this old man here
to return to the land of his fathers.
I haven't come on my own initiative either:
I bear the mandate of my entire people
since it fell to me, by ties of blood,
to mourn his pains as no one else in Thebes.

(728–739)

Creon trades on his blood relation to Oedipus—not a promising note, given the history of such appeals in the Oedipus plays. He also flatters Athens, the "great power," a title with much poignance for the audience of 401 B.C., whose city had recently been thoroughly defeated by Sparta in the Peloponnesian War; and he hides behind his aged frailty, though his henchmen are apparently young enough to use force.

From here the tone begins to turn ugly. Oedipus is called "home" by Thebes, wretched as he is; Creon is "pained" to see him, a "beggar," a "stranger" (*xenos*), stumbling along bereft of sustenance. And Antigone, so frail, so degraded, a young woman still unmarried. Oedipus is a disgrace, to himself and his people;

he can hide himself and avoid further shame by returning to
Thebes (740–759). The attempt to shame Oedipus into com-
pliance fits with Creon's mission and the view of life it represents. Nothing drives the self-sufficient tragic hero like the fear
of appearing inadequate before his fellow heroes. Shame is the
common coin of traditional heroic culture. In Hyde's terms,
Creon appears in the guise of the salesman, looking to move
Oedipus back to Thebes, where the old man will earn a "profit"
for his former city.

The Angry Daimon

Oedipus is moved by this appeal, but not in the way Creon
would hope. As we have come to expect, the attempt to drag him
back into the past enrages and energizes:

What brazen gall! You'd stop at nothing!
From any appeal at all you'd wring
some twisted, ingenious justice of your own!
Why must you attack me so, twice over,
catching me in the traps where I would suffer most?

First, in the old days, when I was sick to death
with the horror of my life,
when I lusted to be driven into exile,
you refused that favor—for all my prayers.
But then, when I'd had my fill of rage at last
and living on in the old ancestral house seemed sweet . . .
then you were all for cutting, casting me away—
these ties of blood you maunder on about
meant nothing to you then.

(761–771)

The tirade continues for another twenty-five lines and we begin to see signs in Oedipus that he has come to feel the new power that closeness to death has brought. He knows the real motives behind Creon's pleas, and they are futile; *he* will tell the destiny of Thebes:

Well that is not your destiny, no *this* is—
my curse, my fury of vengeance
rooted deep in your soil for all time to come!
And for my sons, this legacy: a kingdom in my realm,
room enough to die in—six feet of earth.

Now then, don't I see the fate of Thebes
more vividly than you? Oh so much more,
the sources of all I know are so much stronger:
Apollo and Zeus himself, Apollo's father.

(787–793)

These lines remind us in one sense of Tiresias in *Oedipus Rex*, angered by Oedipus, delivering the true will of the gods. But the cursing has another resonance. In traditional societies, cursing becomes a potent weapon for old men, who draw on their liminal closeness to the gods for power in this world to compensate for diminishing physical strength. And in the specific context of archaic Greek religion, Oedipus invokes the specter of the angry *daimon* the dead hero can become, helping his friends and harming his enemies from beyond the grave, his burial site the center of a cult of anxious worship.

Here we encounter an aspect of the aged Oedipus that defies easy definition and may make us slightly uncomfortable. He is angry, and he is able to contemplate with satisfaction the vengeance he will take from beyond the grave on those who have

wronged him. The anger is consistent with what we have seen
from his other forays into the past, but now it comes with a new
sense of confidence fueled by his growing awareness that he has
a new kind of power *because the gods have a plan for him.* We reflect
that a divine plan for Oedipus is nothing new: that has not
changed— neither for him nor, presumably, for any other mortal in the universe of the plays. What has changed is his awareness of the plan and his acceptance of it. In *Oedipus Rex,* transcendent forces seemed to work against Oedipus's need to feel
powerful by imposing his will on the world around him; now,
by accepting his powerlessness in the face of those forces, he is
apparently empowered to work his will. This hardly looks like
the forming of a new kind of selfless servant of the gods.

What bothers us, perhaps, is that somehow the future defeat
of Thebes looks—to us and to Oedipus—like the fulfilling of
his agenda. So it is, but that is only because the defeat of Thebes
and the victory of Athens are apparently in the gods' plan, over
which, Oedipus has learned through his years of suffering, he
has no control and so must accept, whatever it might be. We may
feel that the distinction between the young, defiant Oedipus and
the old, accepting one would be more telling if he would be
shown to be accepting only of his own suffering, past and present, rather than exulting in the future pain of Thebans. Perhaps, too, we would prefer to think that to move toward death
and thus beyond human life would produce a certain detachment from the grievances of this world.

And so it would, but Oedipus is not now moving in that direction. As long as he is pulled toward Thebes, Oedipus's business
with this world is not finished—he is not ready to die—and as
long as he faces toward the past that Thebes symbolizes, he cannot achieve the final serenity held out to him by the gods. The new
leverage that his knowledge of the gods' plan gives him is here put

in the service of a willful vengeance that reflects the former, heroic Oedipus, jealous of his own prerogatives, quick to accuse others of wronging him. The result is a peculiar mix of attitudes that reflects the still unfinished nature of Oedipus's life journey.

We may pause to reflect further on the role of Creon in this journey. He is, as we have seen, rather a different kind of old man than the Oedipus poised on the edge of the grove. While Oedipus has been wandering, poor and homeless, Creon has been either ruling or standing at the elbow of kings. In this sense, we might well see in him what Oedipus might have become if he had not been forced into self-awareness by suffering. Creon's readiness to resort to shaming and, as we will soon see, bullying tactics fits with the heroic myopia he carries for the Thebans as a whole. *Oedipus at Colonus* is a different play from *Oedipus Rex*, with a looser structure, but in the confrontation of Creon and Oedipus here we can see something of the earlier argument of Oedipus and Tiresias. In each case, an aged foreigner arrives to confront Oedipus with something of himself that he would rather not accept. The difference is that in the earlier play Tiresias points toward a future self, whereas here it is the past Oedipus whom Creon reflects.

Thebes and Athens

Oedipus and Creon continue to trade insults until Creon plays his trump: he has captured Ismene, and will take Antigone, too—hostages to force Oedipus to go to Thebes. The aged chorus are indignant, but neither they nor Oedipus, whose bravado crumbles instantly in the face of these abductions, are able to do much against Creon's thugs as they march off with Antigone. The next seventy lines show an inconclusive standoff, with the chorus attempting to block at least Creon's exit, he threatening war if he is touched. Finally, Creon decides to take Oedipus

himself by force, and the old man resorts to the only weapon he
has, another curse:

> No!—
> let the Powers of this place permit me,
> let me break their sacred silence, one more curse.
> You, you swine—with my eyes gone, you ripped away
> the helpless darling of my eyes, my light in darkness!
> So may the great god of the sun, the eye of the day
> that sees all things, grant you and your race
> a life like mine—blind old age at last!
>
> (864–870)

Creon is undeterred and is on the verge of dragging Oedipus
off himself when Theseus returns—riding a white horse, we
imagine—to thwart the villains.

With Theseus's arrival, the confrontation takes on a further
dimension. Now the standoff is between Athens, home of
democracy and protector of suppliants, and Thebes, the city
that, in the Oedipus plays and in Greek tragedy in general, symbolizes violence and political discord. Both characterizations
were by the time of this play proverbial, but the contrast has an
elegiac resonance here, in Sophocles' farewell to his home. Oedipus initiates the glorification of Athens in his first protest to the
chorus at 258ff.: what good is the city's renown for protecting
strangers if it now expels *him*? The chorus pick up the theme as
Creon tries to drag Oedipus away: "[I]t's the end of Athens,
Athens is no more!" (879). Theseus returns to embody the
virtues of Athens, in contrast to the Theban Creon, who has
shown himself by now to be a thoroughly unpleasant old man.

Hearing the story of Creon's outrages, Theseus sends out a rescue party to intercept the kidnappers, then delivers a stern rebuke:

You, you'll never leave this land until you return
those young girls, produce them before my eyes.
What you've done humiliates me
and your own country, the race that gave you life.
You have come to a city that practices justice,
that sanctions nothing without law, but you,
you flout our authorities, make your inroads,
seize your prizes, commandeer at will!
Tell me, did you imagine Athens stripped of men,
peopled by slaves? Myself worth nothing?

                                   No,
it wasn't Thebes that trained you in your treachery:
Thebes makes no habit of rearing lawless sons.
Nor would she ever praise you if she learned
you're plundering me, plundering our gods,
dragging away their helpless suppliants by force.
Never, I tell you, if I'd set foot on your soil,
even if I'd the most just claims on earth—
never without the sanction of your king,
whoever he might be, I'd never drag and plunder.
I would know how a stranger should conduct himself
in the midst of citizens. But you disgrace a city
that deserves the opposite—your native city, too.
And the fullness of your years that brings you
ripe old age has emptied out your senses.

                                   (909–931)

The generous view of the Theban people as a whole—in
contrast to their unworthy agent—that Theseus offers here has
troubled some students of the play, and has been attributed to
local politics between Athens and Thebes at the end of the Pelo-

ponnesian War. This may well be right, but in any event, the
generosity fits with the picture of Theseus we already have: he,
like Athens, gives the benefit of the doubt. Creon's reply, meanwhile, justifies his bad repute. He never thought Athens un-
manly or unwise. But he also never thought that Athens, noble
bastion of justice that it is, would harbor a parricide, a corrupt
practicer of incest with his own mother. He (Creon) is only one
old man, defenseless, but having a just cause, he will fight back
as best he can (939–959). It is a smarmy performance in the
light of his recent tactics, exemplifying the kind of sophistic,
smooth talker always on the "wrong" side in Greek tragedy, and
putting him yet more firmly in the role of villain, opposed by
the spotless Theseus.

This part of the play is not Sophocles' most subtle dra-
maturgy. The painting of cities and their citizens is in broad
strokes, predominantly black and white; Creon and Theseus in
particular are characters more at home in melodrama than the
normally complex world of Greek tragedy. Theseus dashes onstage three times in this play before the disappearance of Oedipus, each entrance showing him yet more selfless and noble. But
there is no real development of his heroic persona, and we find
in him none of the probing characterization Sophocles uses for
his hero in *Oedipus Rex*. His speeches here are full of virile as-
sertiveness and lofty sentiments; nothing of the darker side of
traditional heroism is evident. Creon, meanwhile, is nasty in an
almost comic-book style: we can imagine him twirling his mus-
tache as he orders his minions to snatch the helpless maidens.
Again, none of the complexity even of the earlier portrait in
Antigone comes through. In this stretch of the play, the goal of
glorifying Athens as the home of justice and moderation seems
to have overridden Sophocles' normally penetrating presenta-
tion of human motivation.

But finally, in any event, this is Oedipus's play, and no other character achieves a very high level of definition. Theseus and Athens on one side, Creon and Thebes on the other, all mirror, on the level in this play most germane to our interests, parts of Oedipus, past, present, future; the future triumph of Athens, already written in the prophecies, signals the gods' will in regard to Oedipus, too: he will realize the fruits of his suffering in his final, Athenian self, and reject the picture of himself that Thebes holds up to him. Both sides tug at the old man, and he stays at the center of our attention, the magnet to which all other characters are drawn. *Oedipus at Colonus* has been a hard play for audiences to warm to, and part of the trouble may be the fact of its peculiar structure: an old man at the center, alternately active and passive, with other characters coming and going in episodic fashion. In this sense, we may see some parallels to the earlier *Electra*, where the emotive but immobile hero responds to the acts of others. Yet Oedipus, though he is present from the play's opening scene until his last exit near the end, is not immobile; his movements, though small in actual distance on the stage, carry enormous symbolic meaning, mapping out his final struggle to be the man he is to be.

Theseus's intervention restores Oedipus, and he launches one more blistering attack at Creon:

Unctuous, shameless—where do you think your insults
do more damage, my old age or yours? Bloodshed,
incest, misery, all your mouth lets fly at me,
I have suffered it all, and all against my will!
Such was the pleasure of the gods, raging,
perhaps, against our race from ages past.
But as for me alone—
say my unwilling crimes against myself

and against my own were payment from the gods
for something criminal deep inside me . . . no, look hard,
you'll find no guilt to accuse me of—I am innocent!
(960–968)

He goes on to review the terrible history one more time:
Laius's murder; the grotesque marriage to Jocasta. This is his
last and most vigorous self-defense, a fierce attempt finally to
establish his innocence by virtue of his ignorance. The gods had
their "pleasure" of him, deciding his doom before he was born,
maybe even settling some ancient grudge against the family: how
can *he* be condemned? Indeed, why is Creon's behavior not worse
than his, since it was done with full knowledge of the circumstances (969–1009)? It is as if Creon's laying hands on him
transmitted some germ of the violent tragic past, and it works
in him now, fueling his sense of being a victim, his relapse into
heroic isolation, a noble man brought low by his "enemies."

Polynices: The Heart of Pain
　　Theseus marches the querulous Creon away, and the chorus,
catching the spirit of force, sing in anticipation of the great battle to come:

O god, to be there!—
where the warring armies wheel and charge—
soon, soon, fighting hand-to-hand
in the brazen cries of battle!
(1044–1047)

They go on for almost fifty lines: Apollo at the pass, Theseus
in the thick of battle, the armed might of Colonus, and so forth.
It is sometimes difficult to catch the exact tone of poetry from

so far away in time, but to me this all seems to be imbued with the melodramatic flavor of the scene preceding. Theseus waylaying a small band of Theban soldiers attempting a shabby kidnapping will not carry the weight this choral ode seems to require. In any event, the reunion of Oedipus with his daughters that follows immediately is founded on firmer emotional grounds:

OEDIPUS:

Child!

You're here, both of you in the flesh?

ANTIGONE:

Yes! His strong arms saved us—

Theseus and his loyal comrades.

OEDIPUS:

Closer, children, come to your father!

Let me embrace you—I never thought I'd feel you,

hold you again.

(1102–1105)

We are reminded of the old man's frailty and vulnerability here, following the thunderous tirade against Creon. He calls his daughters his "supports" (*skeptra*) (1109), and the Greek word has a telling range of associations. It is used to describe both the beggar's staff and the scepter of the ruler in assembly: Achilles slams down the *skeptron* when he leaves the Greek camp at the beginning of the *Iliad*; Odysseus carries a *skeptron* when he arrives at Ithaka disguised as a beggar, then wields it as king after his triumph over the suitors; when Tiresias foretells Oedipus's exile in *Oedipus Rex*, he sees him leaning on a *skeptron*. The image of Antigone and Ismene as the *skeptra* of their father has, then, rich implications. They have been his beggar's staff as he wanders,

but they also perhaps symbolize his return to power on the new
terms decreed by the gods—terms that mandate a more *feminine*
mode of being than his earlier, heroic self.

After mutual shows of affection, Oedipus turns to Theseus
and delivers a passionate speech of thanks, to him and to his city,
where he has finally found "reverence, humanity, and lips that
never lie" (1125–1127). Carried away by his feelings, Oedipus
reaches for Theseus's hand, then checks himself:

> What am I saying?
> You touch *me*? How could I ask? So wretched,
> a man stained to the core of his existence!
> I ask you? Never! I wouldn't let you,
> even if you were willing. No, the only ones
> who can share my pain are those who've borne it with me.
>
>   (1132–1136)

Here is one of the more poignant moments in Greek drama.
Oedipus, outcast and beggar for so many years, finally finds a
new home, and even there cannot have the simple human pleasure
of touch, except from his daughters, who as children of incest
are already, presumably, beyond saving from his polluted soul;
nothing has changed in this regard since the end of *Oedipus Rex*.

Theseus reassures Oedipus, who has apologized for going on
at length: words are not so important to him as actions, and
Oedipus's deeds prove it. But there is one thing. A stranger has
thrown himself as a suppliant on the altar of Poseidon, where
Theseus was sacrificing. Oedipus is immediately curious: Who
is the stranger? What could he want? Theseus says he is from
Argos, and the mood changes instantly. Oedipus wants to hear
no more about the man; he knows him. It is Polynices, "that son
I hate!" (1173). Why not at least *talk* to him, Theseus asks. Be-

cause the very sound of his voice is "loathsome" to his father (1177).

No episode in the play is more controversial than the scene between Oedipus and his elder son. The plot seems to have moved along to some kind of happy ending, with Creon and his nefarious henchmen dispatched, the old man and his daughters reunited. Oedipus has had a chance to defend his past behavior, and even if we are not totally convinced by his claims, at least we feel some sense of closure. To bring on Polynices at this point, retarding the climax of a plot that has already wandered more than is pleasing to some, seems perverse. Though we have seen Oedipus's anger at his sons before, and know its origins, the force of the old man's fury is still daunting. It is a sad thing for a man to hate his children in any event; for Oedipus, it is especially so. Cut off as he is from any connection with his past, threatened with the deadly status of *other*, an old man might look to his children at least for support: the love of children can preserve "object status." This has been possible in the case of Oedipus's daughters, but not with his sons, and in the patriarchal world of the play the difference is telling.

But to yearn for a more tranquil relationship between Oedipus and his sons, for forgiveness instead of unrelenting fury, is to miss the power and significance of what is happening to the old man. Oedipus's isolation is soon coming to an end. In the final, horrific clash with Polynices, the pain of Oedipus's past history is relived and brought to a climax of sorts, in preparation for the great consummation that will mark his departure both from this earth and from the way of understanding himself that helped bring the pain into being.

Against Oedipus's refusal are ranged Theseus, who urges respect for the god on whose altar Polynices has thrown himself, and Antigone, who begins mildly, then hits close:

                    Yes, and you're his father—
so even if he'd inflict on you the worst wrong,
the worst outrage, father, it isn't right
for you to strike back in kind.
                              Oh let him come!
Many other men have rebellious children,
quick tempers too . . . but they listen to reason,
they relent, the worst ones rage in their natures
charmed away by the soothing spells of loved ones.
Look to the past, not the present, consider all
you suffered through *your* father and mother—
look hard at that. You will see, I think,
what a dreadful outcome waits on dreadful anger.
You've good reason to remember, deprived of your eyes—
eyes that can never see the light again.
                              Yield to us!
It isn't good for men with a decent cause
to beg too long, or a man to receive help,
then fail to treat a fellow-victim kindly.

                                          (1189–1203)

   The sentiments are not perhaps startling in themselves—the
need for forgiveness in families, avoiding the same mistakes one's
parents made—but this is not a normal family. She speaks to a
man who not only "suffered" through his parents, he was
marked by them for death—a son who inflicted the ultimate
"outrage" on his father. And, of course, the son who asks for
mercy and forgiveness is also a brother, the daughter who inter-
cedes, a sister. This innocuous-sounding little speech takes
Oedipus to the heart of his painful family life, returning him for
the last time to the past, with all its horrors.
   Oedipus relents, but not without a promise of protection

from Theseus. The Athenian king exits, and the chorus sing their last full song (quoted in part earlier), on the evils of old age. In the final epode, the old men imagine Oedipus as a storm-lashed headland:

This is the grief he faces—I am not alone—
like some great headland fronting the north
hit by the winter breakers beating down
from every quarter—so he suffers,
terrible blows crashing over him
head to foot, over and over
down from every quarter—
now from the west, the dying sun
now from the first light rising
now from the blazing beams of noon
now from the north engulfed in endless night.

(1239–1248)

A faint echo here perhaps of Oedipus's wish at the end of *Oedipus Rex* to live on Mount Cithaeron: "Mother and father marked out that rock/to be my everlasting tomb—buried alive" (1452–1453). The role the chorus projects for Oedipus turns out to be wrong: if there is a storm coming, it will proceed from the old man, and his son is the one to be lashed. The reversal is effective in pointing the contrast between this Oedipus and the kind of man the chorus expects: Sophocles' heroes, whatever else they may be, are never ordinary.

Antigone sees Polynices first, from a distance, approaching in tears. Like the shepherd in *Oedipus Rex*, he walks—slowly, I imagine—across the stage, an emissary from the past. Oedipus remains silent for the first long speech, part of which is addressed to him. We hear at first echoes of Creon, a shocked outcry at the

appalling state Polynices finds his father in. Yet the ugly man-
ner that characterizes Creon's speeches is absent here: Polynices
has wronged his father, and he admits it (1265–1270); he begs
for forgiveness, tells the story of his recent past, and reveals the
reason for his mission: whichever side Oedipus favors in the
coming struggle between him and his brother will win the war
for the throne of Thebes (1331–1332).

Oedipus has maintained a stony silence. The chorus, Antigone, Polynices, all beg him to answer, and finally he relents. The
resulting curse brings to a hair-raising, vitriolic crescendo all of
his previous anger. First, a review of past offenses:

> You, degenerate—
> you, when you held the throne and scepter
> your blood brother now holds in Thebes,
> you drove me into exile, your own father!
> You stripped me of my city, you put on my back
> these rags you weep to see, now, only now
> you've sunk to the same depths of pain as I.
>
> (1354–1359)

He goes on to his years of wandering, begging—all the fault
of his ungrateful sons: only his daughters saved him. Neither
Polynices nor his brother will rule in Thebes; no, they will kill
each other, fulfilling an earlier curse from their father. His last
words to his son spiral into demonic fury:

> *You*—die!
>   Die and be damned!
>   I spit on you! Out!
> your father cuts you off! Corruption—scum of the earth!—
> out!—and pack these curses I call down upon your head:

never to win your mother-country with your spear,
never to return to Argos ringed with hills—
      Die!
Die by your own blood brother's hand—die!—
killing the very man who drove you out!
So I curse your life out!
I call on the dark depths of Tartarus brimming hate,
where all our fathers lie, to hale you home!
I cry to the great goddesses of this grove!
I cry to the great god War
who planted the terrible hatred in your hearts!
Go!—with all my curses thundering in your ears—
go and herald them out to every man in Thebes
and all your loyal comrades under arms! Cry out
that Oedipus has bequeathed these last rights,
these royal rights of birth to both his sons!

                           (1383–1396)

Does Polynices "deserve" this attack? Some readers have painted him in lurid colors, a consummate villain who deserves everything he gets, but finally this seems forced. It appears, in fact, that Sophocles tried to make him as sympathetic as possible in the circumstances. He has been selfish and a bad son, but his abject apologies ring true; he has another agenda, but this does not preclude remorse. There is something monstrous about Oedipus here that no amount of special pleading will ease.

Yet from the perspective we have been developing, the fury, however disturbing, makes sense. Polynices is the last of a series of people who have tried to pull Oedipus back from the grove of the Eumenides; his pleas reanimate the darkest parts of the past; like Creon, he prods at the sources of shame in the old man, and nothing drives anger like shame. In the larger movement of the play, this terrible eruption takes its place beside other angry outbursts that animate the old Oedipus by providing an objective enemy "out there." Such projection, we have said, promotes longevity in old men, and in this context, then, puts off the final walk to his death until his business with this world is done.

In his anger, we have seen Oedipus revert to the way of understanding himself and his life that characterized his earlier, Corinthian persona, as if contact with the past brought his former self back to life. During the exchange between Antigone and Polynices that follows, Oedipus is entirely silent: he will never speak another word to his son. He becomes instead a spectator to a familiar scene: he could be watching himself as a young man—the tragic hero denying the workings of inexorable transcendent forces. Polynices "knows," in the way all tragic heroes know, that his father's refusal to take sides means doom for the expedition against his brother at Thebes. Still he persists — despite the pleading of Antigone—because denial overrides knowledge in the tragic world:

ANTIGONE:
Turn back the armies, back to Argos, quickly!
Don't destroy yourself and Thebes.
POLYNICES:
Unthinkable—
how could I ever raise the same force again,
once I flinched in crisis?
ANTIGONE:
Again? Oh dear boy,
why should your anger ever rise again?
What do you stand to gain,
razing your father-city to the roots?

POLYNICES:

Exile is humiliating, and I am the elder
and being mocked so brutally by my brother—

ANTIGONE:

Don't you see?
You carry out father's prophecies to the finish!
Didn't he cry aloud you'd kill each other,
fighting hand-to-hand?

POLYNICES:

True,
that's his wish—but I, I can't give up.

ANTIGONE:

Oh no . . . but who would dare to follow you now,
hearing oracles the man's delivered?

POLYNICES:

I simply won't report them, not a word.
The good leader repeats the good news,
keeps the worst to himself.

ANTIGONE:

So, my brother, your heart is set on this?

POLYNICES:

Yes—

(1416–1432)

Here the element of projection takes on the flavor of exor-
cism, as if, in his last tirade, Oedipus passes on the poison of
tragic denial permanently to his son, and then watches it work
in him. Now, finally freed of the past, Oedipus can turn toward
the grove again, and make a good death. Polynices, meanwhile,
carries his father's deadly contagion back to Thebes, the symbolic home of all it represents. The episode of Polynices represents a suppliant drama within a suppliant drama, and the out-
comes must differ if Oedipus's spiritual quest is to be fulfilled.

For Oedipus to find a home in Athens, he must deny Polynices—
and the younger version of himself that his son represents—a
home inside himself: the heroic Oedipus must die again to ensure the final coming into being of a different kind of man.

The Last Walk

Everything happens quickly now. Polynices leaves, the chorus's
broodings on time and destiny are cut short by distant thunder.
Oedipus feels the gods calling and sends for Theseus; the thunder comes closer, crashing all around; Oedipus asks again for
Theseus: he would begin to deliver that gift now. The king arrives, noble and timely as always, and hears from the old man
that the thunder signals his imminent death. He has instructions:

OEDIPUS:

I will reveal it all to you, son of Aegeus,
the power that age cannot destroy,
the heritage stored up for you and Athens.
Soon, soon I will lead you on myself, no hand
to lead my way, to the place where I must die.
Never reveal the spot to mortal man,
not even the region, not where it lies hidden.
Then it will always form a defense for you,
a bulwark stronger than many shields,
stronger than the spear of massed allies.

But these are great mysteries . . .
words must never rouse them from their depths.
You will learn them all for yourself, once
you come to our destination, you alone.
I cannot utter them to your people here,
nor to my own children, love them as I do.
No, you alone must keep them safe forever,

and when you reach the end of your own life,
reveal them only to your eldest, dearest son,
and then let him reveal them to his heir
and so through the generations, on forever.

Then you will keep your city safe from Thebes,
the fighters sprung from the Dragon's teeth.
So many cities ride roughshod over their neighbors—
reckless, even if that neighbor lives in peace—
for the gods are strong but slow to see and strike
when a man has flung all fear of god to the winds
and turned to frenzy. Never risk defeat, Theseus,
never divulge what you will learn.
                            Well,
you know these things, no need to preach to you.
On now, on to our destination . . . I can feel
the god within me urge me on—onward,
we must hesitate no more.

                                   (1518–1541)

The transformation has been instantaneous. Frailty is all gone
now, and so is anger. In their place, serene self-confidence: Oedipus is certain that the gods want him to be right where he is,
doing just what he is doing. Along with this new attitude comes
the return of the acceptance that marked his first entrance. We
may say that the drama has returned to where it began, with
Oedipus on the edge of eternity. But with a crucial difference:
what seemed then a sign of frailty is now evidence of a flowering
of the new man; the angry *daimon* has given way to a giver of gifts.

The speech itself is full of poignant meaning—for the
Athenian audience, for us, and (we suppose) for Sophocles himself. Spoken in the wake of Athens's defeat, it has the effect of

offering a different kind of safety for the city—safety not in or from arms and battle but, somehow, in the enduring care of its greatest tragic hero, mysteriously *present* to his adopted home forever. In this context it is impossible to separate the playwright from his creation. Sophocles, too, is close to death, and offers his own gift to the city where he has lived so long: Athens will endure as long as its art remains.

His message delivered, Oedipus rises, walking slowly:

> Follow me, O my children,
> come this way. I stand revealed at last, look,
> a strange new role for me—I am your guide
> as you were once your father's. On, onward!
> No, don't touch me, let me find that sacred grove myself
> where the Fates will bury Oedipus in this land.
> This way, come, walk on! This is the way
> they lead me on, Hermes the Escort of the Dead,
> Persephone, Queen of the Dead.
>
> (1542–1548)

Small physical movements have carried great weight all through this play, but none as much as this slow walk. Until now, Oedipus has been *moved* around the stage by forces beyond his control; now, he leads. In this new vigor and surety, Sophocles shows us the power of the gods coursing through the old man—a physical representation of spiritual transformation. In the longer perspective of both plays, this walk completes a series: Tiresias, the Corinthian messenger, the old shepherd, all arriving in Thebes; Oedipus himself arriving in Colonus, and now finishing the journey by exiting into the grove. Most important are the first and last. Tiresias came delivering and embodying both a past and a future for Oedipus; as he leaves to complete

his long life journey, Oedipus is about to realize the promise that
the old prophet held out to him. Sophocles walks beside the old
Oedipus, and so does Tiresias.

The Great Consummation

As he did in *Oedipus Rex*, Oedipus delivers the hero's farewell
to the light, then leads his daughters, Theseus, and his atten-
dants offstage. The chorus pray to the gods of death to grant
the old man a peaceful end. A messenger appears immediately,
to describe the miraculous end of Oedipus (as so often in Greek
tragedy, acts that redefine the world of the play occur offstage):
Walking into the grove, Oedipus stopped to bathe himself—a
symbolic funeral-washing before the fact. This done, "Zeus of
the Underworld" thundered again, and Oedipus began to say
good-bye to his daughters. This tearful scene is reminiscent of
the end of *Oedipus Rex*: in both instances, a farewell and the beginning of a new existence.

They were interrupted:

> and suddenly,
> a voice, someone crying out to him, startling,
> terrifying, the hair on our heads bristled—
> it was calling for him. over and over,
> echoing all around us now—it was some god!
> "You, you there, Oedipus—what are we waiting for?
> You hold us back too long! We must move on, move on!"
>
> (1623–1628)

Deities appear on stage and talk to mortals frequently in
Greek tragedy, but this disembodied voice is unusual. And so is
the plural "we," as if Oedipus had already passed into the com-

pany of the gods. One more set of embraces for his daughters, a
plea to Theseus to protect them, and then he was gone, taking
only the king with him to witness:

That was the last we heard him say, all of us
clustering there, and as we followed the daughters
sobbing, streaming tears . . . moving away we turned
in a moment, looked back, and Oedipus—
we couldn't see the man—he was gone—nowhere!
And the king, alone, shielding his eyes,
both his hands spread out against his face as if—
some terrible wonder flashed before his eyes and he,
he could not bear to look. And then, quickly,
we see him bow and kiss the ground and stretch
his arms to the skies, salute the gods of Olympus
and the powers of the Earth in one great prayer,
binding both together.
                But by what doom
Oedipus died, not a man alive can say,
only Theseus, our king.
No blazing bolt took him off,
no whirlwind sweeping inland off the seas,
not in his last hour. No, it was some escort
sent by the gods or the dark world of the dead,
the lightless depths of Earth bursting open in kindness
to receive him. That man went on his way,
I tell you, not with trains of mourners,
not with suffering or with sickness, no,
if the death of any mortal ever was one,
his departure was a marvel!

                                          (1645–1665)

Though other mortals are deified in Greek literature, there is nothing like this strange and wonderful exit. The gesture of Theseus, binding earth and heaven together in prayer, fits the mood here of wholeness, completion. We do not know where Oedipus has gone, only that he has been taken there by and in the company of the gods, only that his long life has reached a closure somehow marked by the divine. The play continues for another one hundred lines or so, as the living try to understand and absorb what has happened, but nothing more can be known about the old man's death. Theseus, dutiful to the end, has sworn to keep the mysteries secret, and we hear no more of it in ancient literature. Oedipus, in his last moments, has become the gift that circles into mystery, to the source that is inexhaustible. And with him go Sophocles and Tiresias, all part of the circle of giving that will someday come back around to Athens: the spirit of the gift increases because the body of the gift is consumed.

Conclusion: Wholeness

Endings create form, and form points to meaning. Thus the last line of *Oedipus Rex*: "count no man happy till he dies, free of pain at last" (1530). Now Oedipus has "died," whatever that can mean in the context of his mysterious exit. What meaning can we find, in the play and in the life it dramatizes? Beginning with the play, we can see a three-part structure. The first two hundred lines or so show the old man poised on the edge of his life, symbolized by the boundary of the grove. He is passive, accepting, frail, and he looks forward to finding rest. Then his past begins to intrude in various ways, introduced by the curiosity of the chorus and Ismene's news about his sons. From here until Polynices exits, the play is dominated by the struggle to pull Oedipus back into the Theban past, with all its consequences. In this long middle section, Oedipus plunges back into the world, animated by his hostility; he is assertive, angry, and willful. The final third begins with the gods' thunder, when Oedipus turns away from Thebes and the past and toward the grove of the Eumenides, animated as before, but now by the power of the gods running through him like divine electricity.

If there is a "meaning" to this structure, it is that Oedipus is not ready to leave this world until he confronts his past once more; that to make a good death, he must finish his business with life. Doing so brings risk, because the past is toxic for Oedipus, drawing him back not only to a painful set of events but also to a way of understanding himself that somehow stunts him spiritually. In the present, what might be a gift looks to him like a burden; in the future he envisions, a vengeful *daimon* looms, not a mysterious member of the gods' giving circle.

It is important to recognize the element of *choice* in Oedipus's behavior in his last hours. Oedipus is ready to accept the gods' will for him and others at the beginning of the play, and his attitude seems consistent with the implications of his self-blinding. But moral character is always founded finally on personal choice, even if it means choosing to accept. In his struggles with Creon and Polynices, we see Oedipus asserting himself, reentering his past to state his case. When he is facing in this direction, we also see him stepping backward into the role of aggrieved victim that fits with his earlier heroic persona, and not with his more mature, accepting self. But finally, he chooses the present, chooses to turn his back on his past self and even on his own sons, with all the horrific consequences for them and Thebes. This done, he can turn toward the grove and walk serenely to his fate. Here, as in *Oedipus Rex*, coming to spiritual maturity is not without its costs for Oedipus. *Oedipus at Colonus* is not about how old age can be without pain—accepting the will of the gods gives no guarantee of that. It is about how living the truth as best we can know it, whatever the consequences, makes us whole.

The particulars of the old man's exit also point to the complex interaction of knowledge, will, and power that we have used as a way to approach the problem of finding meaning in a life. Realizing in his death his role as giver and gift, Oedipus finalizes a new bond with Athens and with all of the cosmos. What comes to fruition then is a new configuration of self-in-the-world—a change that became possible after the self-blinding. The heroic perspective is founded on an understanding of the self as a discrete entity, acting out into an external, objective "reality." Identity is confirmed in this view by the integrity of the boundaries of the self: separation leads to self-creation; autonomy is the goal of self-realization. The aged Oedipus challenges this model. Transcendent forces have shaped his fundamental identity in ways over which he has had no control. His acceptance of this truth is first signaled by the self-blinding, but the implications of such a perspective are not explored until the later play. Trudging into view in the first scene, he presents a vivid picture of what exactly the gods and fate have made: a tired old man, worn out by wandering. That he accepts his suffering seems there to be as much a sign of his weakness as of wisdom. Striding serenely into the grove at last, he shows us a different kind of man—powerful *because* of his acceptance. Between these two walks, we have seen the two personae alternate, following the rhythm of the plot.

The key to Oedipus's eventual triumph lies in the achieving of what modern metaphors call passive mastery. Blinding himself, he cut himself off from the agency characteristic of young heroes, turning toward the inner vision embodied by Tiresias; the new power he taps is another kind of agency, and implicit within this new role is a redefinition of the relationship between self and other. The old man is empowered by accepting his powerlessness in the face of transcendent forces; he becomes a channel for these forces. His identity follows, then, from his role within a larger system; it is not, as before, the product of his detachment from other parts of that system. To put it another way, self-realization is no longer measured by autonomy.

The metaphors of giving offer the sharpest focus for this new configuration. As an agent for the gods, Oedipus enters into a gift circle with the Athenians. As Hyde reminds us, taking part in such a circle offers the possibility of expanding the boundaries of the self; as the gift moves, the self can go with it: "There is a consciousness in which we act as part of things larger even than the race" (17). Oedipus not only offers a gift to the Athenians, he *is* the gift. Passing from the earth, he fully assumes the kind of identity we have been tracing here. His disappearance is mysterious; it leaves us with the strong sense of inclusion and completion, symbolized in Theseus's prayerful gestures. What has been completed is the making of Oedipus. His identity is now fully integrated into the larger forces of the cosmos: he is whole.

Metaphors of cosmic unity dominate most spiritual systems, representing the final goal of the human quest for completion. Because the dominant heroic model of identity works against wholeness, linking self-realization with a discrete, autonomous self, being gathered into the divine can only be understood from the heroic perspective as an obliteration of the person in the larger and unknowable cosmos—not completion but dissolution. *Oedipus at Colonus*, if we listen carefully, is telling us something different: only by recognizing our oneness with the universe do we become the person we were always meant to be. This is Sophocles' final answer to the question posed by the riddle of the Sphinx.

CONCLUSION

Ancient Heroism and the Meaning of a Masculine Life

All things end in the Tao
as rivers flow into the sea.

Lao Tzu, *Tao Te Ching*

According to quantum mechanics there is no such thing as objectivity. We cannot eliminate ourselves from the picture. We are a part of nature, and when we study nature there is no way around the fact that nature is studying itself.

Gary Zukav, *The Dancing Wu Li Masters*

It is only the time lag and the immense complexity of the relations between stars and men which make it difficult to see that they imply one another just as much as man and woman, or the poles of the earth.

Alan Watts, *Nature, Man and Woman*

We learn from the life of Oedipus how the meaning of a traditional masculine heroic life, as it is experienced from within, is bound up in issues of power and identity. Returning for a moment to some fundamental distinctions that lie behind ideas about "meaning," we observe that, like the Greeks, we normally understand form as prerequisite to meaning, formlessness as meaningless: "cosmos" simply means "order." Form is in turn

157

defined by limit, or boundary: "to define" means "to put a boundary around." Implicit in the idea of boundary is an inside and an outside. To put it another way, meaning demands a context, something within which it resides. The sources and guarantors of this meaning must lie "outside" it in some sense, transcendent in time, space, or essence. Thus we have some difficulty in talking about the creation of the universe: what was outside it, bringing it into being by imposing limits? In the beginning of Hesiod's characteristically Greek cosmology was Chaos, "formless emptiness"; the world "begins"—that is, there is a temporal boundary; hence, meaning—when some shape is created *within* this undifferentiated matter by the apparently spontaneous generation of the first two deities, Earth and Eros (Hesiod, *Theogony* 116–122). But this still leaves the pesky question of what defines Chaos. Our own cosmologies eventually come to the frightening issue of the shape of the universe: If there is an outer edge to everything that is, what can lie beyond that? (Einstein's model of curved space has not yet, I think, quite taken hold in the minds of most.) If there is *no* boundary to the universe, what does it "mean?" Infinity (lack of boundary) is without meaning.

Likewise, the meaning of a life depends, in this model, on form. I understand the creature "I" to exist within certain boundaries—spatial, temporal, psychic, spiritual. Here is where identity and the meaning of life intersect: I am myself within the bounds of my self; to determine the meaning of *my* life, I must first know where I end and the rest of the cosmos begins. My life has a beginning, middle, and end; move the end up close, and every act has meaning; slide it way out into the distance, and things lose their urgency, and ultimately their meaning. In this perspective, human life, like everything else we can understand as meaningful, has a context: the ultimate sources of meaning in a human life are those that are beyond it, transcendent—nature, the gods, "fate." (For the existentialist, who discerns no shape in what transcends human life, meaning is somehow created from the *inside* of the boundary, by acting outward into the world, like blowing up a balloon. But the balloon needs something pushing back against the air inside to have shape—problems here.)

Following from the fundamental apprehension of *form* as prerequisite to a meaningful life is the feeling that one's life has meaning if it has a purpose. I am leading a meaningful life if I am here, now, for some *reason*—if my life is shaped by some sense of a goal. If I reach my goal, I have fulfilled my "potential"; that is, if I have tapped the power to which the purpose in my life gives me access. Already, in the word "shape," we see the link to form. Purpose implies an end, which in turn implies a limit; because my life is seen to have a finite shape, taking up a certain space, it appears to have some meaning. Returning to the thought experiment above, if we remove the boundaries of an individual life, meaning is drained out of it. The Greek gods have unlimited power and unlimited time; therefore, nothing they do in their own sphere (as opposed to the mortal world of time and change) matters; their lives have no purpose or meaning in themselves. The "potential" of a life suggests a power to be developed, the realization of which we see in our physical selves if not always in our emotional or spiritual selves: the gods, in and of themselves, have no potential, since they are already all-powerful. To mean something, we must *move* in some dimension, be it temporal or some other; but finally, the sense of movement is satisfying because it implies a goal, a boundary, a shape.

Oedipus Rex offers a powerful meditation on the ideas we have been reviewing here. In particular, the play dramatizes the peculiar heroic way of seeing the connections between identity and meaning. Oedipus, when we meet him in the beginning of the play, seems a conventionally pious man, with respect for the power of the gods. But when we look at the assumptions behind what he says and does, a different picture emerges—one of a man who believes that he creates the shape, and so the meaning, of his own life by acting outward. The can-do attitude he adopts toward kingship reflects this assumption, as if there were no problem that the application of his intellect, driven by his will, could not solve. This attitude is founded, in turn, on the assumption that there is a fundamental separation between the world "out there" and Oedipus. And *this* boundary seems firm to Oedipus because he understands himself—that is, his self— as coextensive with his ego, the conscious captain of his will.

Now the mosaic falls into place: the Corinthian Oedipus, whom the king of Thebes understands, can stand apart from the riddle of the Sphinx or the plague and act against the firm boundaries that separate his identity from these manifestations of the "other." And—here is the key—by doing so, he seems to carve out a shape for his life, and so creates meaning in it. The most seductive part of this model is the way the heroic, self-cre-ated life seems to have meaning insofar as the ego-driven will feels powerful. In other words, by expressing power over what is separate from me, I am creating purpose and meaning in my life, and so I am becoming the person I am to be. Small wonder that this perspective has proved so irresistible over the centuries.

The depth of Sophocles' grasp of these patterns is clear from the way he exposes them for us. When Oedipus is confronted by his other life, his other self, all of the masculine, heroic struc-tures of meaning are challenged. The "other"—that is, the The-ban—Oedipus has been formed by transcendent forces beyond his control: here is a version of himself that does not mirror back to him his power over the rest of the universe. Meeting this new man and knowing him to be part of himself, the heroic, Corinthian Oedipus finds that the vehicle for that sense of power— his autonomy, marked by the discrete boundaries between his self and the rest of the cosmos—is compromised, because the boundaries have been breached: his identity has suddenly been pulled into the larger context of nature, divine will, and fate; the plague is not "out there" but inside him. And not only does his identity change, but also the meaning of his life. From godlike maker of meaning, he "descends" to the level of something made, the meaning of which has sources beyond him.

Modern Heroism

The explosion of technology in this century is driven by the same masculine model of selfhood to be found in ancient heroic stories. As we have learned to manipulate the natural environment, the illusion of control over nature through intellect has flourished, reaching a glorious crescendo of sorts in the space program of the 1960s and 1970s, but continuing apace in computers and biogenetic engineering. The gains from this revolution have been dramatic: cures for disease, increased capability of prolonging life, early warning for potentially fatal weather, and so forth. But recently we have begun to see the darker side of this control, in the destruction of the environment, the destruction of people, and the debilitating alienation and loneliness of modern life. And yet, though the dangers in embracing the heroic myth become clearer each day, we find it hard to let go of or even modify this way of understanding ourselves and the meaning of our lives.

Sophocles tells us why: it is not just that we cannot let go of the excitement and material comfort afforded by technological advances, but also that, once we occupy the heroic self, we cannot find meaning in life without it. The bargain that this way of seeing ourselves offers is alluring, but finally Faustian. To control the world, we must be separate from it; the illusion of control makes us feel powerful, and with that feeling comes the feeling of personal authenticity and a meaningful life. But heroism also isolates us, so we feel vulnerable; to protect ourselves against the hostile world "out there," onto which we have projected all the dark parts of ourselves, we reach for more power, which isolates us further, so we build more prisons and more weapons, which make us feel powerful and safe, but alone.

The market economy, a method of organizing societies that is ever more ascendant in the modern world, is predicated on the heroic model of selfhood, in which maximizing my "earning power"—that is, my power over others—maximizes my personal authenticity. This may help to explain the seeming puzzle of people—indeed, whole nations—starving amid material abundance. In *The Gift*, Lewis Hyde makes the connection between heroic autonomy and what he calls the Law of Scarcity that informs modern capitalism (23):

Given material abundance, scarcity must be a function of boundaries. If there is plenty of air in the world but something blocks its passage to the lungs, the lungs do well to complain of scarcity. The assumptions of market exchange may not necessarily lead to the emergence of boundaries, but they do in practice. When trade is "clean" and leaves people unconnected, when the merchant is free to sell when and where he will, when the market moves mostly for profit and the dominant myth is not "to possess is to give" but "the fittest survive," then wealth will lose its motion and gather in isolated pools.

The profit that stays behind in pools when goods move is used to buttress the self-created boundaries of the heroic prisonhouse of the self, while at the same time creating threats to that self in the form of desperate, starving people, which in turn requires more power to protect the alienated self—which is the basis for identity and meaning underlying the whole system to begin with. Our common way of speaking about human interaction reflects the tenacity of this way of seeing ourselves in relation to others, and reminds us of its *gendered* qualities. To be excessively confined within the bounds of oneself is to be "selfish"; to nurture, to reach out to others across the boundaries of the self is to be "selfless." Since nurturing is often considered in this view to be "feminine," then to be feminine is to dilute the boundaries of the self, to lose identity.

We have come to a remarkable place: for my (masculine) life to have meaning, I must be powerful; to be powerful, I must be alone, but at the same time surrounded by people with whom I must not share my "goods," lest the boundaries of my identity be blurred. Indeed, the presence of those who envy and perhaps hate me is proof not only of my success and power, but also of my identity, and the proper goal of *their* lives is to achieve a similar position with regard to others. Here we find the modern analogue to the seductive, but ultimately destructive, bargain between the hero and his community in ancient heroic narratives.

Given its self-perpetuating nature, it is not surprising that those who start down the path of heroic self-creation find it hard to turn aside: we may, like Oedipus, have to be forced off the road. It appears in fact that there may be a natural rhythm informing our susceptibility to the lure of the masculine hero myth, that we eventually meet evidence of other voices in other rooms, and are ready to hear them. The story of Oedipus shows us that we may respond by choosing another way of understanding ourselves that acknowledges our inclusion in a larger arena of meaning.

The Second Half of Life

Oedipus turns inward when he blinds himself. Doing so, he voluntarily lets go of the *agency* that characterized his heroic separation from the cosmos. The facts of his birth and early history have already undermined that position, placing him firmly within the context of time, nature, and death. Now he symbolically chooses to explore what it means to be made as well as maker, to grow into the new self that his past presents. The blindness brings an increased sense of vulnerability; that Oedipus *chooses* it shows—from our perspective here—his decision to trust in powers beyond himself to keep him safe. This is a major break with the assumptions of the heroic model of the self, which responds to vulnerability by strengthening the barriers that keep others out. The years of wandering—reflecting the disengagement characteristic of the midlife transition—aptly represent a period of exploration, of rootlessness as a state of receptivity to whatever gifts life has given or will give.

His sons have turned away from him, pursuing their own self-created heroic fantasies by denying their biology, and he leans on his daughters, his *skeptra*. Appropriately enough: to move from active shaper to passive sufferer is to shift—in the Greek view and (still) in ours—from a masculine to a feminine mode of being; to embrace voluntarily the feminine, which the Greeks understood to be attuned to the rhythms of nature as opposed to culture, is in turn to imperil the boundaries of the autonomous self, the sources of meaning in a heroic masculine life. The consequences of Oedipus's choice throw into relief the sources of the Greek male's fear of women: to be in the world of women is to risk loss of self, oblivion, through inclusion: Calypso, the threatening female of Odysseus's journeys, gets her name from the verb *kalypto* ("I smother"); she offers Odysseus

immortality, the seductive but ultimately meaningless existence
of the gods.

The collapse of boundaries when Oedipus meets his other self
also has, as we have seen, implications for his understanding of
himself as a moral agent. As hero, he projected onto others those
parts of himself that could do harm. Now it turns out that the
criminal lives inside him, and cannot be kept at a comfortable distance; the outlines of moral issues, once clearly focused by their
objective distance from the masculine hero, now turn fuzzy. The
drama of choice, always central to our understanding of character,
now moves its venue from the outer edges of the hero, surveying
the field of possible externalized targets for action, into the
murky inner recesses, sorting through impulses that may be
frighteningly dark. Now the masculine insistence on *rights*, to protect the boundaries of autonomous moral agents, must make
room for the "feminine" ethic of reaching across boundaries to
care for others—including oneself—with its focus on *responsibility*.

All of this follows from Oedipus's decision to blind himself.
By the end of *Oedipus Rex*, then, we already have before us some
signs of how the meaning of a masculine life can begin to evolve
in midlife. The central theme is of *inclusion*, and the challenge this
process presents to the primacy of being a maker instead of
something made. Faced with the fact of our powerlessness before forces that lie beyond our control, we may make various
choices. We may decide to fight against the fact of our immersion in larger orders, in all or some of its manifestations: age has
not slowed me down—I can hold off physical decay by exercis-
ing more; the troubles I am experiencing are not mine, but the
work of some new set of "enemies" out there; I do not need to
lean on friends, but to work harder. Denial has many forms, and
offers seductive if temporary relief. But if we choose instead to

learn from Oedipus, to begin by accepting the fact of inclusion, the meaning of our lives changes.

Made as well as makers, we begin to understand power differently. Our characteristic mode of experiencing power passes from McClelland's stage three, in which we are the source of power that we impress on the world "out there," to stage four, in which we are neither source nor object, but feel powerful insofar as we seem to be a channel for a higher source. Such a reorientation fits with the reconfiguring of identity that follows from inclusion. The shape of my self is not now entirely of my own making; its boundaries are determined by powers over which I never had control. Now the meaning of my life is dependent not on what I make and do, but *where I fit* in the larger order of things; perhaps I can realize the purpose of my life by living out the contours of what I have been *given*.

These changes in turn encourage a subtle shift in our evaluation of the importance of autonomy in the meaning of life. Since I have not, apparently, entirely made myself or the shape of my life, perhaps I do not need to be afraid to let go of the illusion of control: many things never have been under my control, and I have made it this far, so why not relax? Maybe I can be safe even if I do not control the world. This is the equivalent of Oedipus's decision to choose to trust the universe by blinding himself. And if my autonomy is not needed to keep me safe, then I can perhaps guard my "rights," and the rules that guarantee them, less zealously. Instead I can think about how my part in larger structures makes my identity more dependent on recognizing my responsibility to others. I can think less about what separates me from others and more about how I am connected to them; perhaps who *I* am is a function not so much of my autonomy as of my interdependence with the rest of the cosmos; perhaps my "self" expands with the gift I pass on.

The Last Day

Oedipus's—and Sophocles'—last day on the Athenian stage reviews the entire shape of the hero's life. *Oedipus at Colonus* dramatizes outwardly, in the movements of the old man toward and away from the grove, what can also be understood as an inner struggle to realize the fruits of the original decision to turn inward. Because Oedipus is on the threshold of death, the struggle is given intensity: the ultimate shape, and therefore meaning, of his life is about to be decided. If Oedipus turns back toward Thebes, with all that it symbolizes, he reenters the self-destructive world of traditional heroism and the narrow model of self that world implies. So when he plunges into the past, to reexamine and defend his actions, or to face those who would pull him back, we see a man at home in the heroic milieu: angry at others, whom he believes have caused his pain, projecting the parts of himself and his past that do not fit with his selective idea of who he is—a long-suffering victim—out onto the people "out there."

We may see what looks like a paradox here. The habit of externalizing sources of pain is associated in modern studies of old men with longevity. So cursing, the most potent weapon of old men in traditional societies, turns out to be "healthy"; so when Oedipus is in his combative, heroic mode, finding enemies onto whom he can project his darkness, and with whom he can frighten himself, he is behaving in a way that is apparently "good for him." And it is, if we accept the heroic idea that death is an enemy, the ultimate *limit* to be avoided at all costs. But the old Oedipus does not arrive in Athens looking to prolong his life. On the contrary, he is looking for the right place to die. The mode of being that he has been experiencing while wandering all those years has a different hierarchy of imperatives than the heroic life. The horrendous curses he unleashes against his "enemies" in the course of the play *do* prolong his life, in that they keep him turned away from the place where he knows he must eventually go. But to live on is not anymore the primary objective; now to die in the grove of the goddesses is "good for him."

How can this be? Though we may "see" in an intellectual way how this conclusion might be reached from a reading of the plays, the strength of the heroic perspective in our lives makes it hard to accept wholeheartedly the idea that death is "good." If someone is terminally ill and in great pain, then maybe death is better than living: "It was a blessing." Otherwise, we usually feel that there is something wrong with those who *want* to die. To die is, for the hero, the ultimate loss of control: the isolated "I," agent of all that creates meaning, ceases to be. It is no surprise that modern science has taken as one goal the ability to prolong life at any cost. But as we have seen, the new model of being-in-the-world that follows from the crisis of inclusion at midlife has a larger notion of the boundaries of the self. Whatever "I" am is within the context of other, transcendent forces and structures of meaning. Why, indeed, is death not seen to be a part of the larger process of which we are one manifestation? Why is death not a part of "me"?

The Meaning of Oedipus's Life

The disappearance of Oedipus completes the shape of his life as we at least can know it: the battle to determine the meaning of that life is finished. What can we say about its final form? The gesture of Theseus is one of *connection*, as if something in the old man's departure binds together what we ordinarily see as separate: sky and earth, spirit and flesh. In this connectedness we see boundaries erased, wholeness established—or perhaps reaffirmed. The *completion* of Oedipus's life is realized in his ultimate immersion in the cosmic order, personified by the gods who call to him as a companion, but comprising finally all that is. So ends what we like to think of as a metaphorical journey. Oedipus has traveled far in the two plays: from lonely isolation to cosmic inclusion; from tightly bounded masculine ego to an expansive, more feminine self that binds heaven and earth in a gift circle; from heroic defier of time and change to part of the endless ebb and flow of eternity. We, as fellow travelers, may perhaps see in the journey something familiar. Our heroic will to control and shape nature, our defiance of death, our struggle to fortify the boundaries of our egos, all reenact ancient urges. And we may, if we choose, finally turn away from the lure of these forces and walk with the blind old man into the embrace of eternity.

FURTHER READING

Introduction

On the Oedipus myth and its afterlife in literature, see Edmunds 1985. Studies of the hero story are myriad. The most comprehensive treatment of the *masculine* hero story is still Campbell 1949. See also Van Nortwick 1992. For an introduction to the issue of gender as it relates to the life cycle, see also May 1980; Gilligan 1993. For traditional humanist views of the tragic hero in Sophocles, see Whitman 1951, Knox 1957 and 1966. Segal 1986, chapters 1–3, gives a helpful overview of more recent theories, such as structuralism, semiotics, and deconstruction as they are applied to Greek tragedy; Segal 1981, 1–42, is a more detailed discussion of the structuralist approach. Vickers 1973 argues convincingly for the accessibility of Greek tragedy to modern audiences, differing with other modern interpreters who have stressed the alien qualities of the genre (e.g., Jones 1962; Lloyd-Jones 1983). For a lively and informative view of the fifth century B.C.E. in Athens, see Beye 1987, 97–125. Vernant and Vidal-Naquet 1988 gives a brief but stimulating set of remarks about the intersection of historical circumstance and mythical form in Athenian tragedy, and Knox 1957, 53–106, sets *Oedipus Rex* within the intellectual context of the fifth century. Goldhill 1986, 197–243, is a more specialized study of the centrality of language as a subject in the intellectual life of Athens, and Segal 1993, 3–11, 36–43, offers good summaries of the cultural and historical context for the performance of Athenian tragedy.

Psychological studies of the Oedipus figure begin with Freud, whose most influential statement about the "Oedipus Complex" comes in Freud 1965, 294–296. Pucci 1992 gives a good overview of the problems and issues raised by Freud's original ideas, plus an update on the more recent theories. See also Vernant and Vidal-Naquet 1988, 29–48, 85–111; Segal 1993, 57–63. On the application of Jung's theories to the study of literature, see "The Origin of the Hero" in *Symbols of Transformation* (*Collected Works, vol. 5*); "The Phenomenology of the Spirit in Fairytales" in *The Archetypes and the Collective Unconscious* (*CW* 9.1); "Psychology and Literature" in *The Spirit in Man, Art, and Literature* (*CW* 15); *Aion: Researches into the Phenomenology of the Self* (*CW* 9.2). See also Van Nortwick 1992, 3–5; Stevens 1983.

On the psychology of aging, still a relatively new field, see Gutmann 1975, 1977; Neugarten 1977. For the psychology of the life cycle more generally, see Levinson 1978; Gould 1972; Lowenthal, Thurnher, and Chiriboga 1975; McClelland 1975.

Chapter I

The scholarship on *Oedipus Rex* is enormous. What I list here—a fraction of the work that has been done on the play—includes only those works that are directly relevant to what I cover in the chapter. General studies accessible to the nonspecialist: Reinhardt 1979, 94–134; Whitman 1951, 122–148; Knox 1957; Kirkwood 1958; Cameron 1968; Gould 1970; Gellie 1972, 79–105; Vickers 1973, 495–525; Segal 1981, 207–248; Scodel 1984, 58–72; Segal 1993. The problem of Oedipus's identity is central to my work here. Particularly helpful on this topic are Knox 1957; Cameron 1968; Pucci 1992.

Oedipus Rex is structured around riddling, puns, and the role of language as a key to identity; for more on this topic, see Knox 1957; Segal 1981, 241–244; Vernant and Vidal-Naquet 1988, 113–140; Goldhill 1986, 205–221. For more on the figure of Tiresias, see Reinhardt 1979, 104; Segal 1981, 241; Gellie 1972, 84–86; Segal 1993, 104–109.

Chapter 2

For more on the significance of the reversals in the last part of *Oedipus Rex*, see Knox 1957, 185–196; Winnington-Ingram 1979, 179–204; Vernant and Vidal-Naquet 1988, 113–140; Segal 1993, 114–133. On the hero and the life cycle, see Mc-Clelland 1975, 1–76; Levinson 1978; Stevens 1983, 140–173; Van Nortwick 1992. Oedipus's self-blinding has drawn much attention from interpreters, especially those with an interest in the psychological implications of the act, on which see Devereux 1973; Caldwell 1974. The best general introduction to the phenomenon of blindness in ancient Greek culture is Bernadaki-Aldous 1990.

Chapter 3

The scholarship on *Oedipus at Colonus*, though not as formidable as that on *Oedipus Rex*, is still daunting. Again, I will mention only those works directly relevant to my ideas here. This chapter is an expansion of my earlier article on *Oedipus at Colonus*, Van Nortwick 1989. The most useful general studies of the play are Whitman 1951, 190–218; Knox 1966, 143–162; Gellie 1972, 159–173; Winnington-Ingram 1980, 248–279; Segal 1981, 362–408. Blundell 1989, 226–259, gives valuable background for the moral substructure of the old Oedipus's behavior; see also Easterling 1967; Burian 1974. Bernadaki-Aldous 1990, 135–232, provides a detailed reading of the play with special

attention to Oedipus's blindness. On old age in classical literature, see Falkner and deLuce 1989. I had not yet read Falkner's
brilliant analysis of the play, Falkner 1995, when I wrote this
book. I am delighted to see that my ideas are consistent with his.

Chapter 4

The meeting between Oedipus and Polynices has been the
most controversial part of the section of *Oedipus at Colonus* covered in this chapter. For more, see Whitman 1951, 210–212;
Knox 1966, 158–162; Easterling 1967; Burian 1974. The
meaning of Oedipus's disappearance has evoked less response
than might be expected, given its uniqueness within Greek literature. Thoughtful assessments can be found in Reinhardt 1979,
219–224; Whitman 1951, 214–218; Knox 1966, 160–162;
Segal 1981, 402–405.

Conclusion

The ideas in this chapter are all elaborations of a fundamental paradigm that finds expression in many places. The most accessible (and enjoyable) reading on this perspective is found in
the work of Alan Watts. In particular, see Watts 1953, 1966.
Zukav 1979 gives a different slant, incorporating the findings
of the "new physics."

BIBLIOGRAPHY

Ahl, F. 1991. *Sophocles' Oedipus: Evidence and Self-conviction*. Ithaca: Cornell University Press.

Bernidaki-Aldous, E. 1990. *Blindness in a Culture of Light*. New York: Peter Lang.

Beye, C. 1987. *Ancient Greek Literature and Society*.[2] Ithaca and London: Cornell University Press.

Bloom, H. ed. 1988. *Sophocles' Oedipus Rex*. New York and Philadelphia: Chelsea House Publishers.

Blundell, M. W. 1989. *Helping Friends and Harming Enemies*. Cambridge: Cambridge University Press.

Burian, P. 1974. "Suppliant and Savior: *Oedipus at Colonus*." *Phoenix* 28: 408–429.

Caldwell, R. 1974. "The Blindness of Oedipus." *International Review of Psychoanalysis* I: 207–218.

Cameron, A. 1968. *The Identity of Oedipus the King*. New York: New York University Press.

Campbell, J. 1949. *The Hero With a Thousand Faces*. Princeton: Princeton University Press.

————. 1971. *The Portable Jung*. New York: Vintage Books.

Devereux, G. 1973. "The Self-blinding of Oedipus." *Journal of Hellenic Studies* 93: 36–49.

Easterling, P. 1967. "Oedipus and Polyneices." *Proceedings of the Cambridge Philological Society* 193:1–13.

Fagles, R. 1984. *Sophocles: The Three Theban Plays*. New York: Penguin Books.

Falkner, T. 1995. *The Poetics of Old Age in Greek Epic, Lyric, and Tragedy*. Norman, Oklahoma: University of Oklahoma Press.

Falkner, T., and J. deLuce. 1989. *Old Age in Greek and Latin Literature*. Albany, New York: State University of New York Press.

Freud, S. 1965 *The Interpretation of Dreams*. Translated by J. Strachey. New York: Avon Books.

Gellie, G. H. 1972. *Sophocles: A Reading*. Melbourne: Melbourne University Press.

Gilligan, C. 1993. *In A Different Voice*. Cambridge, Mass: Harvard University Press.

Goldhill, Simon. 1986. *Reading Greek Tragedy*. Cambridge: Cambridge University Press.

Gould, R. 1972. "The Phases of Adult Life: A Study in Developmental Psychology." *American Journal of Psychiatry* 129. 521–531.

Gould, T. 1970. *Oedipus the King*. Englewood Cliffs, N.J.: Prentice Hall.

Gutmann, D. 1975. "Parenthood: Key to the Comparative Psychology of the Life Cycle?" in *Life-Span Developmental Psychology: Normative Life Crises*. Edited by N. Datan and L. Ginsberg. New York: Academic Press.

———. 1977. "The Cross-Cultural Perspective: Notes Toward a Comparative Psychology of Aging" in *Handbook of the Psychology of Aging*. Edited by J. Birren and K. Schaie. New York: Van Nostrand and Reinhold.

Heath, Malcolm. 1987. *The Poetics of Greek Tragedy*. Stanford: Stanford University Press.

Hyde, L. 1979. *The Gift*. New York: Vintage Books.

Jones, J. 1962. *On Aristotle and Greek Tragedy*. London: Chatto and Windus.

Jung, C.. *Collected Works* [1902–1958], vols. I–19. Princeton: Princeton University Press.

Kirkwood, G. 1958. *A Study of Sophoclean Drama*. Ithaca: Cornell University Press.

Knox, B. 1957. *Oedipus at Thebes*. New Haven: Yale University Press.

————. 1966. *The Heroic Temper: Studies in Sophoclean Tragedy*. Berkeley: University of California Press.

Lattimore, Richmond, trans. 1951. *The Iliad of Homer*. Chicago and London: The University of Chicago Press.

Levinson, D., *et al.* 1978. *The Seasons of a Man's Life*. New York: Ballantine Books.

Lloyd-Jones, H. 1983. *The Justice of Zeus*.[2] Berkeley: University of California Press.

Lowenthal, M., M. Thurnher, and D. Chiriboga. 1975. *Four Stages of Life*. San Francisco: Jossey-Bass Publishers.

Martindale, C. 1993. *Redeeming the Text*. Cambridge: Cambridge University Press.

May, R. 1980. *Sex and Fantasy*. New York: Norton.

McClelland, D. 1975. *Power. The Inner Experience*. New York: Irvington.

Merton, T. 1968. *Conjectures of a Guilty Bystander*. Garden City, N.Y.: Image Books.

Neugarten, B. 1977. "Personality and Aging," in *Handbook of the Psychology of Aging*. Edited by J. Birren and K. Schaie. New York: Van Nostrand Reinhold.

Pucci, Pietro. 1992. *Oedipus and the Fabrication of the Father*. Baltimore: Johns Hopkins University Press.

Reinhardt, Karl. 1979. *Sophocles*.[3] Translated by Hazel Harvey and David Harvey. Oxford: Basil Blackwell.

Scodel, R. 1984. *Sophocles.* Boston: Twayne Publishers.

Segal, Charles. 1981. *Tragedy and Civilization: An Interpretation of Sophocles.* Cambridge, Mass.: Harvard University Press.

————. 1986. *Interpreting Greek Tragedy: Myth, Poetry, Text.* Ithaca: Cornell University Press.

————. 1993. *Oedipus Tyrannus: Tragic Heroism and the Limits of Knowledge.* New York: Twayne Publishers.

Stevens, A. 1983. *Archetypes: A Natural History of the Self.* New York: Quill Books.

Van Nortwick, Thomas. 1989. "'Do Not Go Gently . . .': *Oedipus at Colonus* and the Psychology of Aging," in Falkner and deLuce 1989, 132–156.

————. 1992. *Somewhere I Have Never Travelled: The Second Self and the Hero's Journey in Ancient Epic.* New York: Oxford University Press.

Vernant, J. P., and P. Vidal-Naquet. 1988. *Myth and Tragedy in Ancient Greece.* Translated by Janet Lloyd. New York: Zone Books.

Vellacott, Philip. 1971. *Sophocles and Oedipus.* Ann Arbor: University of Michigan Press.

Vickers, Brian. 1973. *Towards Greek Tragedy.* London: Longman Books.

Watts, Alan. 1953. *Nature, Man and Woman.* New York: Pantheon Books.

————. 1964. *Beyond Theology.* New York: Pantheon Books.

————. 1966. *The Book.* New York: Pantheon Books.

Whitman, Cedric. 1951. *Sophocles: A Study of Heroic Humanism.* Cambridge, Mass.: Harvard University Press.

Winnington-Ingram, R. P. 1979. *Sophocles: An Interpretation.* Cambridge: Cambridge University Press.

Zukav, G. 1979. *The Dancing Wu Li Masters: An Overview of the New Physics.* New York: Morrow.

INDEX

179